Parikshita Awaiting
And
Siddhartha The Other
(Two Plays)

Parikshita Awaiting
And
Siddhartha The Other
(Two Plays)

Ananda Chandra Pahi

Translated by
Sanjeet Kumar Das

BLACK EAGLE BOOKS
Dublin, USA | Bhubaneswar, India

Black Eagle Books
USA address:
7464 Wisdom Lane
Dublin, OH 43016

India address:
E/312, Trident Galaxy, Kalinga Nagar,
Bhubaneswar-751003, Odisha, India

E-mail: info@blackeaglebooks.org
Website: www.blackeaglebooks.org

First International Edition Published by
Black Eagle Books, 2025

PARIKSHITA AWAITING AND SIDDHARTHA THE OTHER TWO PLAYS
by **Ananda Chandra Pahi**

Translated by **Sanjeet Kumar Das**

Original Copyright © Ananda Chandra Pahi
Translation Copyright © Sanjeet Kumar Das

All rights reserved. No part of this publication may be reproduced, stored in a retrieval system, or transmitted, in any form or by any means, electronic, mechanical, photocopying, recording or otherwise without the prior permission of the publisher.

Cover & Interior Design: Ezy's Publication

ISBN- 978-1-64560-690-1 (Paperback)

Printed in the United States of America

*To the people who love
to read and stage plays
in the world.*

Author's Note

There was a time when four different commercial theatre troupes in Odisha staged various plays. Some of these theatrical works gained immense popularity among the audience and ran successfully for months. This provided incredible motivation for playwrights to write new plays. The audience eagerly awaited new productions. However, those days are gone. The commercial theatre troupes collapsed, one after another, for multiple reasons.

A particular query often arises about our plays. It is said that from 1960 to 1965, Odia plays followed a specific trend. After that, a phase of experimentation began, like a gust of wind. Plotless, abstract, and obscure plays were written in the name of experimentation and were staged as well. The audience watched them with patience for some time due to their novelty but eventually failed to comprehend them. Consequently, the audience rejected them, and the craze for experimental plays gradually faded away. Now, it's great to see that the trend of story-based, realistic, and artistic plays has returned. Today's theatrical works are able to please and mesmerize the audience with their soulful artistry and organic craft. The audience is once again drawn to the auditorium, just like in the old days.

These plays are not intended only to be staged. It is unanimously agreed that, like other genres of literature such as short stories, novels, articles, and poetry, these plays can be read with great relish. Social issues can be showcased beautifully and powerfully through these dramas, just as they are through short stories and novels. The same degree of pleasure can be attained while reading these plays as is derived from short stories and novels. Despite this, the number of plays available in Odia literature is relatively less than in other genres.

Now, let's look at our Odia literature magazines. Most magazines generally publish short stories, poetry, novels, and articles. Notable literary magazines for children are also published, especially with children's stories and poems. There are special magazines solely for short stories too. However, there is not a single Odia magazine exclusively meant for plays or one-act plays, nor is there any provision for their publication in any magazine. This demotivates young writers from creating new plays, and as a result, the number of plays in Odia literature has relatively decreased.

The publication of these plays or one-act plays certainly has its own complications, but the bigger challenge lies in performing them on stage. The disintegration of permanent theatre troupes is the main reason why it is now a hassle to stage a newly written play with the same ease as before. So, the manuscripts remain with the playwrights, waiting for years without ever being performed. Of course, a few plays are staged by some fancy institutes, cultural clubs, schools, and colleges. But there is no proper arrangement to ensure the manuscripts reach them smoothly. Institutes in search of new plays never get a play of their preference. Meanwhile, the manuscripts remain idle with the playwrights and never see the stage. We are yet to find a connecting link between them. The possibility of finding such a link within a time frame seems impossible to predict.

If there were a magazine exclusively published for plays, it would be possible to print those manuscripts and bring them to the attention of theatre lovers. In this way, the magazine could serve as a great connecting link between playwrights, directors, and theatre troupes.

Theatre troupes could find plays of their choice from that magazine. We can assume that if such an exclusive magazine for plays were published monthly, it would automatically help increase the number of plays written. This could help at least five to seven plays every month reach directors, theatre troupe actors, and actresses. I sincerely hope and believe that this could bring a revolutionary change in the field of theatre.

However, some plays and one-act plays are being broadcast on radio and television. The number of such plays also varies due to several factors.

The tradition of converting a good story or novel into a play or cinema no longer exists in Odisha. The practice of assigning an efficient playwright to develop the screenplay of a movie is dwindling. A great number of formula movies in the Odia language, mostly inspired by Hindi and Telugu movie industries, are being produced and screened now. Nobody recognizes the role of a playwright in writing the screenplay for such movies. That's why the artistic quality of Odia films is deteriorating. Some time ago, a few new Odia movies based on original Odia stories were produced and released in cinema halls. They were widely accepted and appreciated by the audience. This endeavor is truly praiseworthy.

Our state has a long-standing tradition of performing plays on stage at the annual day functions of schools, colleges, and universities. But nowadays, no school, college, or university follows this tradition. Instead of plays or one-act plays, institutions perform melodies of Hindi songs. If the government would pay attention to this by ensuring that these educational institutions perform Odia plays and one-act plays on the eve of their annual function days, it could certainly motivate the staging of more Odia plays and one-act plays. This could create a platform to showcase at least five to seven thousand plays on stage every year. As a result, students would revive their interest in writing and staging plays from their school days.

There is certainly one more point to note here. There will be significant growth in the publication of books related to plays if the government takes an interest in purchasing books on Odia plays and one-act plays for the libraries of schools, colleges, and universities.

The most crucial point here is that the number of books translated from Odia into other languages is less than one-hundredth of a percent of the books translated from English, Hindi, Telugu, and Tamil into Odia. This is a matter of regret. In this context, I would like to thank the director of Black Eagle Books, U.S.A, Sri Satya Patnaik, who has shown interest in publishing English translations of our Odia short stories, novels, poetry, and plays and has taken the responsibility to place them on international platforms for wider readership. I am grateful to him for publishing my translated work on time at his esteemed publishing house.

I would also like to thank Mr. Sanjeet Kumar Das, Assistant Professor, Department of English Language and Literature, Central University of Odisha, for translating two of my Odia plays into English sincerely and wonderfully without deviating from the original tone and temperament.

Ananda Chandra Pahi

Translator's View

Ananda Chandra Pahi is one of the prominent playwrights of Contemporary Odia Literature. Here, I have translated two of his award-winning Odia plays, *Pratikshare Parikshita* and *Anya Eka Siddhartha*, into English as *Parikshita Awaiting* and *Siddhartha the Other*, respectively, for the global readership.

Since time immemorial, it has been commonly observed that the higher species of animals imitate others either of the same or of other species, and so are human beings. This process is genetically encoded in their blood and accepted worldwide. While establishing a symbiotic relationship with Nature, the people stayed together peacefully. Then, there was the need of society. The cultural mores or norms are devised and handed down from generation to generation and sometimes amended occasionally to socialize with other community members. Thus, the culture wherein we breathe our life is never fixed but always dynamic to suit best the needs of the hour and the interests of the public. The fundamental principles that govern God-made Nature and Man-made Society are the 'Principle of Asymmetry' and the principle of Dependency'. Then, one feels that others' presence in society is vital. These two principles are also interrelated. If we ponder the asymmetry principle, we can see an absence of some trait in the individual or the society. Then, the 'Principle of Dependency' plays its role. We unanimously agree that we all are interdependent. We think about the future generation and the healthy social life. We share some means of education and entertainment with other community members. Then, the literary pieces, maybe fictional or fact-based, are penned down by the writers to galvanize the public sentiments.

Here, the plot of the play *Parikshita Awaiting* is based on social realism, how a small kid gets affected by the incidents happening in the surroundings every day, and fear engulfs the senior most persons in the family and society. I have stated above that culture/ society/environment shapes an individual. Parikshita, the play's protagonist, and other family members, like two sons, Sandeep and Pradeep and wife, Shashwati, are sprayed by the fear complex at home. This fear factor engulfs the entire family members when Parikshita opens the letter inserted in the door stating, 'Your head will be severed from the body'. That was written by a child, Chintu, a classmate of Parikshita's younger son, Pradeep. He writes it out of anger. But the family members and neighbours think that a hardcore criminal or goon has chalked out this evil plan carefully.

Fearful of the situation, the family members buy weapons like daggers, minor axes, choppers, and staffs from the market and store them at home. The mystery of this story is revealed towards the end of the play. As one grows older year by year, one becomes mature, complex, and simultaneously fearful while living in society. One more point we should bring to the knowledge of each citizen is that our daily newspapers, T.V. channels, social media, cinemas, and surroundings cite heinous crimes proliferating and aggravating in society. The kids are severely affected by the incidents in rural or urban areas. They plan to commit such crimes over trivial issues without their parents' knowledge. This is what exactly Chintu does in the play. The play ends with a strong message that we, the people, are all responsible, or our responsibility is to safeguard society from this evil turmoil. We must be watchful to closely guard our youngsters to march on the path of righteousness for a better and brighter state and nation. Society is responsible for teaching anything good or harmful to youngsters. The entire neighbourhood of Parikshita is indirectly disturbed by such an incident. The playwright also highlights the solipsistic attitude of city people. They are always ready to provide advice and suggestions. The suspense is retained until the play ends. The resolution is also theatrical, as Chintu, instead of any other criminal or terrorist, is found to have threatened his friend Pradeep in Parikshita's family. Then, family members are incredibly terrified and quite helpless, and their tension is released the day Chintu is nabbed by Pradeep and Sandeep outside his home and brought to the family, where the neighbours gather to resolve the issue. The adage 'Much cry and little wool.' can be aptly applied here.

The protagonist, Siddhartha, in the second play, *Siddhartha, the Other*, makes the people aware of the life they have been blessed with on this planet. He doesn't discuss salvation, nirvana, moksha, or enlightenment like Goutam Buddha. Here, he advocates for the people on Earth to focus on the work that will make them immortal. In this play, Siddhartha, the only son of the industrialist Rajendra, leaves his father, fiancée Lopa and friend Sambit to meditate in the dense forest full of wild creatures of the Mountain of Himalayas. Rajendra, Lopa, and Sambit, accompanied by security personnel, have followed him since he ran away from home. While meditating, he visits heaven in his dream and meets the God of Wealth, Kubera and Agni Deva, the God of Fire, and finally, Vishnu, God the Almighty. Siddhartha asks them, "How can the people on Earth attain the immortal life you all experience here in heaven?" Their answers bring out the new changes in Siddhartha's life. Where there is no death, there is no life. There is nothing new. No changes are marked in the life. Our ever-youthfulness and eternal spring in heaven make our life monotonous and disappointing. We have been suffering this life since time immemorial as if cursed. But the people on Earth like you think that we enjoy life here. Variety is the beauty of life that you all experience there. Sometimes, some of us step down to Earth and get thrilled. Initially, he requests the Almighty to bless the people with *jatismara*(the power to recollect their past lives). But later, he understood the repercussions of that.

Jatismara is a curse. The merits of being *jatismara* are also interwoven with demerits. Through this stage, we will carry experience, perseverance, and perfection on one side and sorrows, plights, and issues on the other as baggage of erstwhile lives. The *Jatismara* people will have no fear of death. Fearless life is indisciplined. Lord Vishnu's reply transformed him entirely: "One must do some work on Earth during one's lifespan for which that person will be remembered forever or immortalized. There will be no plights of eternal life nor tiredness but pride and glory of immortality. When there is a rush of immortal lives on Earth, that planet will be converted into heaven. Nobody will come to heaven for immortal life."

This Siddhartha's message to society is as follows : "This Earth is beautiful and unparalleled. Here, sorrow beautifies and glorifies happiness, darkness to light, old age to the youth, and death to life. Not fearing death, one should continue noble and virtuous deeds within one's short life span. That work will make the people immortal."

The above mentioned message is unlike Gautam Buddha's noble truths: "1. Life is full of suffering; 2. Desire is the cause of suffering; 3. The end to desire leads to the end of suffering and the attainment of enlightenment/ nirvana."

Gautam Buddha moves away from his family and society to mediate in the dense forest. This Siddhartha returns from the forest to his love Lopa, father Rajendra and friend Sambit. He advises society on how they can be immortal in this life here on Earth. Hence, the title *Siddhartha, the Other* is justified in the text emblazoned herewith.

While translating the Odia plays of the playwright into English, the 'Principle of Equivalence' and 'Principle of Faithfulness' between the Odia language and the target language, English, are carefully considered. I came across some natural shifts. I have translated these texts into English using language as lucid as possible for a better understanding of the commoners to have a grip on the aesthetic beauty of the regional language. Some collocational expressions of the source language are with glosses in parentheses in translation.

I want to thank the playwright Ananda Chandra Pahi for having faith in me to translate two of his Odia plays into English.

I convey my heartfelt gratitude to Satya Pattanaik, the director of Black Eagle Books, U.S.A., and Sri Ashok Parida of the publishing house for their kind consent and timely action in publishing the work of art on time.

Sanjeet Kumar Das

Parikshita Awaiting

Dramatis Personae

Parikshita	:	A Class-III Government Officer
Shashwati	:	Parikshita's wife
Sandeep	:	Parikshita's elder son
Pradeep	:	Parikshita's younger son
Nabin	:	Parikshita's Neighbour
Prasant	:	Parikshita's Neighbour
Dilip	:	Parikshita's Neighbour
Naresh	:	Newspaper Hawker
Jyotish	:	Astrologer
Chintu	:	Pradeep's classmate
Somnath	:	Sandeep's uncle

SCENE- I

[Parikshita is a Class-III government employee. It is evening at his government residence. A tape recorder in the drawing room is playing a Hindi pop song. Parikshita's eight-year-old son, Pradeep, is busy break-dancing to the tunes. Towards the end of the dance, his elder son, Sandeep, a college student, enters.]

Sandeep : (Stands for a while to watch Pradeep's dance and then claps) Wow, you dance really well!

Pradeep : (Stops dancing and switches off the tape recorder.) I hope you won't tell Dad about this.

Sandeep : Do you know that Michael Jackson is world-famous for his dancing? Why are you so scared? Is dancing a crime?

Pradeep : No, but I have pending homework. Twenty-five complex time and work-related math problems gave me a raging headache. Both Mom and Dad went to the temple and told me to stay at home and finish the work.

Sandeep : A little dance in the middle of solving math is okay. Otherwise, continuous math calculations can drive you insane. These days, teachers don't think. Just imagine, how can a small child like you solve twenty five tough math problems in one day? They don't have time to understand that. And on top of it, there are continuous tuitions, one in the morning, one in the afternoon, one in the evening, and then once again at night.

Pradeep : Our teacher takes tuition four times in a day.

Sandeep : Leave it. Let's not talk about your teacher. Just hum the lyrics of that hit Prabhudeva song 'Muqabla, muqabla'' and dance your heart out.

Pradeep : I don't remember that song. You sing, I will dance.

Sandeep : I don't remember it either.

Pradeep : A new Govinda movie released at Keshari Talkies today.

Sandeep : Who told you it is released today?

Pradeep : Why should someone tell me? I read it in the newspaper.

Sandeep : Not today, it was released last Thursday. I already watched it with my friend, Tapan. This movie has an amazing fight scene. And that innovative fighting style turned this movie into a blockbuster.

Pradeep : An amazing fight scene?

Sandeep : You are just a child. Watching those fight scenes can mentally disturb you. Just go ahead and continue with your dance.

Pradeep : No, why don't you tell me more about the fight?

Sandeep : Like I said, you are just a child. If you watch that scene, you might go crazy.

Pradeep	: Govinda is the hero in that movie. How could he fight? He is a dancer. Have you seen Sanjay Dutt fighting?
Sandeep	: I have seen all of them fighting. From Sanjay, Shahrukh, Salman, Aamir, Akshay, and Sunil Shetty to Hrithik Roshan, Tiger Shroff and Ranveer Singh.

(Parikshita and Shaswati return from the temple at that time with an offering plate in hand)

Parikshita	: Who have you seen fighting?
Sandeep	: (Unprepared and uneasy) No, no, it's nothing. I was just lying to Pradeep.
Shashwati	: Come, take this *bhoga* (food offered to God).

(Sandeep and Pradeep receive the *bhoga* offered by their mother.)

Parikshita	: Hey Pradeep! Have you finished solving the math problems?
Pradeep	: No, Dad.
Parikshita	: (Angrily) What is this 'No, Dad'? Your teacher is going to check them tomorrow. What will you do if you don't finish them?
Sandeep	: Dad! I saw him doing math for a long time.
Parikshita	: If he was working on them, why couldn't he finish?
Sandeep	: These are tough questions, Dad. Both of us tried to solve them together.
Pradeep	: Yes, Dad! The questions are tough. I couldn't solve them. So I asked Bhai (Brother) for help and he also could not solve them.
Sandeep	: Nowadays, the teachers...they don't teach anything, and the syllabus is extremely demanding too.

Parikshita	: Show me the ones you could not solve.
	[Pradeep and Sandeep look at each other.]
Parikshita	: Why are you standing there like fools? I asked you to show me the question you couldn't solve. Why don't I see your books and school bags here? How were you solving the math problems without them?
Pradeep	: My books and bag are here only, Dad!
Parikshita	: I know you have your bag and books. But show me where they are.
	[Pradeep goes to the other room to bring the school bag.]
Parikshita	: Hey! Why are you going to that room?
Pradeep	: To bring my school bag.
Parikshita	: If you were solving math in this room, then why are your books and bag lying in the other room?
Pradeep	: So what? Is it impossible to solve math here even if my school bag is lying in the other room?
Parikshita	: How is it possible?
Pradeep	: Wait! Let me think for a while.
Parikshita	: What is there to think about? Just tell me how you did it.
Sandeep	: Pradeep had learned the math question by heart.
Pradeep	: Yes, he is right. I remembered that question. We were discussing it.
Parikshita	: Oh! You were discussing! What do you mean? Math isn't like literature or history that you can just talk about. It needs to be solved with pen and paper. I don't see any pen or paper here.

Sandeep	: Dad, you know these math problems are way more advanced than what you had to deal with. And we aren't as clueless as your generation.
Parikshita	: (Gets Angry) Are you trying to say that we are fools? Do you mean we are stupid and you all are the intellectuals? Is this the kind of knowledge you have gained from going to school? How can you call your father a 'fool'?
Sandeep	: (In frightened tone, stammers) D..D..Did I say that?
	(Shashwati enters)
Shashwati	: What kind of drama is going on here? Both of you go to your rooms and continue your studies. Hurry up!
	(Pradeep and Sandeep go to the other room.)
Shashwati	: Will they ever listen to you if you argue with them like this?
Parikshita	: They must listen to me, or else I'll thrash them soundly.
Shashwati	: Physical punishment is now a thing of the past. They will go off track if we don't guide them in the right direction.
Parikshita	: Leave that to me. I will find a way to bring them back on track. You don't need to interfere in this matter. Could you please hand me today's newspaper?
Shashwati	: (Brings the newspaper after searching for it in the room) Take this.
	(Parikshita reads the newspaper. Shashwati gets busy in organizing things in the room.)
Parikshita	: (Reads the newspaper) Complaints lodged against illegal tips collection. The illegal tips

collections has been carried out forcefully in all the districts, including Cuttack city. The police have arrested eight individuals for stealing scooters and motorbikes from people who refused to pay these tips. Terror of militants in Kashmir. Ruffians have set a shop on fire. Two young men arrested in connection with a gang rape incident. A hooligan has threatened to kill a family within four days.

Shashwati : It looks like there is no other news except crimes, theft, rape and robbery.

Parikshita : (Raises his head from the newspaper) How can it be? Theft, robbery, murder, rape, hooliganism are usually occurring in every nook and corner of our country. Newspaper is just a reflection of that.

Shashwati : Reading this kind of news repeatedly can cause panic and agitation. It's better to step away. Please stop reading your newspaper. Why don't you go get some wheat and kerosene from the ration shop?

Parikshita : Give me the Ration Card and shopping bag.

Shashwati : (With ration card and bag in her hand) Take this. Check the wheat before buying. Don't buy if chaff or insects are present.

Parikshita : I am no longer a school boy, so please don't teach me. I have my own eyes to see and check.

Shashwati : Had you been so good at checking things, then why would I have lectured you unnecessarily?

Parikshita : Bickering is your hobby. You can't get rid of that.

Shashwati	:	Just leave, or else you will be late and the shop will close.
Parikshita	:	Ok, I am going.
Shaswati	:	Come back early.
Parikshita	:	Now, this is why I get irritated with you.
Shashwati	:	Why? What did I do?
Parikshita	:	Don't you know?
Shashwati	:	No!
Parikshita	:	I have not even left the house; and you expect me to come back early.
Shashwati	:	So, what's wrong in that? Wherever you go, your chitter-chatter with others doesn't stop for hours.
Parikshita	:	You see, it's closing time at the shop and nobody will be there to chat with.
Shashwati	:	Okay, do as you wish. We are totally out of sugar and wheat. Hurry up! Otherwise, the shop will close.
Parikshit	:	Okay, I am leaving. (Parikshita exits with the ration card and shopping bag in hand.) (Light off)

SCENE- II

[The location is Parikshita's government accommodation. It's early morning. You can hear a hen clucking outside. The doorbell of Parikshita's main door rings.]

Parikshita : (Wakes up from bed and yawns) Who the hell is ringing the bell so early in the morning? One can't even sleep peacefully.

Shashwati : Looks like it is Prabha at the door. Why are you staring at me? I am talking about your younger sister, Prabha.

Parikshita : This is not a convenient time for Prabha to come.

Shashwati : What is inconvenient about the timing? Whenever she comes, it is always at this time. The bus from Koraput arrives in Bhubaneswar early in the morning.

Parikshita : I am not talking about the timing. How can she come when there are no holidays?

Shashwati : Then, go and check who it is.

Parikshita : (Gets up from bed stretching and yawning) My sleep is disturbed so early in the morning. Who knows what kind of misfortune awaits my day?
(He goes to the door, opens it, and looks around.)

Shashwati	:	Who? Who has come?
Parikshita	:	No one is here.
Shashwati	:	Go outside and check. There must be someone.
		(He goes outside and comes back.)
Parikshita	:	No, no one is outside.
Shashwati	:	No one? (She verifies again and finds a chit of paper stuck to the door.)
Parikshita	:	Show me, where did you get this paper from?
Shashwati	:	It was pasted on the door.
		(She gives the paper to Parikshit.)
Parikshita	:	(He opens up the folded paper) Get me my glasses, Shashwati!
Shashwati	:	(She hands over the glasses to him from the table). Read it, let's see what is written inside.
Parikshita	:	(In a state of shock) Oh no, what is this? Who has written this?
Shashwati	:	What's written?
		(Parikshita appears tense and begins to tremble with fear.)
Shashwati	:	Why are you shivering like this? What happened? What's written there?
Parikshita	:	(While sobbing) We are ruined, Sandeep's Maa! Everything is finished. I have never harmed anyone, who has written a letter like this?
Shashwati	:	(Starts crying) Why are you behaving insane? What's written there? Please tell me.
Sandeep	:	(Wakes up from sleep) What happened, Mom?
Pradeep	:	Why is Dad so worried?

Shashwati	:	What's the matter? What's there in the letter?
Parikshita	:	(Hands over the letter) Take this and read it yourself.

[She takes the letter from Parikshita's hand and hands it to Sandeep to read. Both Shashwati and Pradeep eagerly peek at the paper.]

Shashwati	:	Read this. Let' see what is written inside.
Sandeep	:	You will be beheaded within seven days.
Shashwati	:	(Howls) What are you saying? Who will be beheaded?
Parikshita	:	Who else? It's me obviously.
Shashwati	:	Don't utter such inauspicious words.
Parikshita	:	Who else you think is threatened when the letter is inserted into my door?
Shashwati	:	Have you harmed any one? Why do think some one will kill you?
Sandeep	:	Dad! Do you ever had enemies?
Parikshita	:	To the best of my knowledge, I have neither harmed anyone nor made any enemies.
Sandeep	:	(Inspects the paper from all the sides) There is no name mentioned. Who would have sent this?
Shashwati	:	It was pasted on our door.
Parikshita	:	Do you think people who make threats will ever reveal their identity? He wants to remain anonymous; otherwise, he would have confronted us directly to intimidate us.
Shashwati	:	What do we do now? I am really scared. I can feel the panic within me. (She starts shivering with fear.)
Parikshita	:	I can't think of anything. Oh Lord Jagannath! Hey Chakadola! What sort of trouble is this?

		(He suddenly sits on the sofa, and covers his head with his hands.)
Shashwati	:	How can you sit there with the door wide open? I'm worried someone might enter the house. Go and shut the door immediately. Hurry up, don't just sit there like a dump on a log.
Parikshita	:	Sandeep! Go and shut the door, tightly! My body feels completely frozen.
		(Sandeep fastens the door latch.)
Pradeep	:	Dad, go and hide under the bed in that room. No one will be able to find you there. We won't disclose anything to anyone. If that man can't find you, how can he harm you?
Shashwati	:	You just go from here Pradeep! Please go.
		(Shashwati pushes Pradeep towards the other room.)
Sandeep	:	I suspect this might be the work of terrorists. They are extremely dangerous.
Shashwati	:	Who are they?
Sandeep	:	You never read the newspaper. How will you know them?
Shashwati	:	So what? If you explain, I will definitely understand.
Sandeep	:	I recall reading in the newspaper about eight days ago that a gang of terrorists had entered Odisha. They are extremely brutal. I believe this might be their doing.
Shashwati	:	We have not harmed them. Why would they kill us?
Sandeep	:	They are terrorizing the entire country, and killing hundreds of innocent people triggering bomb blasts and firing gunshots.

	It's not about somebody's fault. They just want to kill people mercilessly to create panic.
Pradeep	: (Enters) *Bhai* (brother)! Do they look like the Yogi?
Sandeep	: Why did you come here again? Just go back to your room. (Sandeep pushed Pradeep from behind. Unwilling, Pradeep reluctantly returned to his room.)
Shashwati	: Sandeep! Do they forcefully enter houses to kill people?
Sandeep	: Yes, mom! They enter the house and kill the entire family. They lack sympathy or mercy for anyone.
Shashwati	: Oh, Mother! Oh, my God! Hey Jagannatha!
Parikshita	: Why will the terrorists threaten me when there are already so many people in Odisha? Besides, it is not their role to threaten. They shoot in public to instill fear among the crowd.
Shashwati	: Then, who do you think has threatened us? We don't have any conflict with anybody in this colony.
Parikshita	: No, we don't.
Shashwati	: We didn't have any conflicts with anyone at our previous colony either.
Parikshita	: No, we didn't.
Sandeep	: Dad! Just try to remember if you had any kind of dispute at your office.
Parikshita	: No, I didn't.
Sandeep	: Any kind of disagreement? Not even a small squabble?

Parikshita	:	No. I can't recall any such incident. My colleagues at the office may seem fierce as bears and tigers on the outside, but in reality are quite gentle. They are like a flock of sheep crammed into a cowshed called 'Office'. Their friendship and rivalries are all pretenses, they don't think from the heart.
Shashwati	:	Then, who else can it be?
Parikshita	:	I am not able to guess.
Sandeep	:	Can you identify this handwriting?
Parikshita	:	No, I can't. Besides, the person who sent this letter wouldn't write it himself. He's not a fool. I believe this letter was written with great caution. Special care was taken to make the handwriting unidentifiable. It seems the letters were not written with the right hand but intentionally with the left hand. (The door bells rings.)
Parikshita	:	(Agitated) See, he has come. Sandeep, get me something. (He gets up).
Shashwati	:	(Stops Parikshita) No. You don't go there. I am shivering.
Pradeep	:	(Enters) Dad? Who is it?
Parikshita	:	(With a choked voice) He... He... The... The... one who has threatened us. It's he. Sandeep! Go get me something to defend ourselves.
Sandeep	:	(In a strained voice) What? What do I get you?
Parikshita	:	(With a choked voice) Get... Get... me something.
Sandeep	:	Mom! Get me something.
Parikshita	:	Hurry up! Stop standing like this. Get me a weapon.

Shashwati	:	Weapon? What sort of weapon?
Parikshita	:	A staff.
Shashwati	:	Do we have a staff?
Parikshita	:	Get me a small axe then.
Shashwati	:	We don't have an axe.
Parikshita	:	A dagger? At least?
Sandeep	:	Dad, I have told you many times to get us a dagger, but did you ever buy one? You just buy whatever you feel like. Do you ever listen to us?
Parikshita	:	Don't we have anything at home for such kind of emergencies?
Shashwati	:	You have never given priority to buying weapons before, so why are you searching for it now? (The doorbell rings again.)
Parikshita	:	Get me anything that is available at home, Sandeep's Mom! Get it fast.
Shashwati	:	I don't have anything except the vegetable chopper. You want that?
Parikshita	:	Get me that! Hurry up!
Shashwati	:	Wait, I will get it from the kitchen. (Goes to the kitchen)
Parikshita	:	Hurry up!
Parikshita	:	You stay here Sandeep! (Pushing Sandeep aside) No, you don't go there. I will go.
Shashwati	:	(Enters) Take this. (She hands the vegetable chopper to Parikshita. Parikshita slowly but cautiously marches towards the door.)
Parikshita	:	Oh, My Lord Jagannatha, Baliyarbhuja, save me!

Shashwati	: (Pulls Parikshita from behind) No! Don't open the door.
Parikshita	: If we delay any longer, he will force his way into the room.
Sandeep	: Dad! Just ask who is there.
Shashwati	: Yes, yes. Ask him. (In a strained voice)
Parikshita	: (Gulps his saliva) Yes, you are right. It is very dangerous to open the door without asking. When a man is in fear, he loses his common sense. Who's there?
Shashwati	: (Whispers) Little louder.
Parikshita	: (Loudly) Who… Who's there?
Naresh	: (From outside) It's me.
Parikshita	: Who are you?
Naresh	: I am Naresh.
Parikshita	: (He asks Sandeep and Shashwati in a low voice) Who is Naresh?
Shashwati	: I don't know.
Sandeep	: Me, neither.
Parikshita	: Naresh who?
Sandeep	: (In a rising tone) We don't know any Naresh.
Shashwati	: (In a low voice) Don't be so harsh. If he gets angry, he will break the door.
Sandeep	: Terrorists usually break through the door to enter, but they prefer to come by motorbikes or vehicles. We haven't heard any vehicles arriving.
Parikshita	: They might have kept it away, somewhere at a distance.
Naresh	: (From outside) Please open the door, Sir. I am the newspaper hawker.
Parikshita	: Newspaper hawker? No, it's not his voice.
Shashwati	: No, he is not our newspaper hawker.

Sandeep	: Terrorists are skilled at altering their voices. They use different tones and pitches to suit various occasions.
Naresh	: (From outside) Paresh Bhai has gone to our village. I am his younger brother, Naresh.
Sandeep	: Yes, Dad! He sounds like the younger brother of our newspaper hawker.
Parikshita	: Do you know him? I hope he is not a terrorist.
Sandeep	: No. He is the one who distributes the newspaper in his brother's absence. You can open the door now.
Parikshita	: (Asks Shashwati) Then, I am going to open the door.
Shashwati	: Okay, do it.
	[Parikshita opens the door. Naresh enters.]
Naresh	: (He hands over the newspaper.) Bhai had instructed me to collect the monthly dues. Your due for this month is one hundred and fifty rupees.
Parikshita	: You may go now. I will pay your brother when he comes back.
Naresh	: Yes, Sir.
	[Naresh leaves. Parikshita Babu shuts the door immediately.]
Parikshita	: Oh, no... we are afraid of this bloody newspaper hawker now!
Shashwati	: He has already left. Why are we talking about him? You please concentrate on recalling who else might threaten us.
Sandeep	: Yes, Dad! Please try to remember.
Parikshita	: Who else could it be? I don't know many people in this big city. The only ones I know are the three flat members of our building,

	my colleagues at the office, the milkman, the newspaper hawker, the man at the salon, and the salesperson at the grocery shop. I don't know anyone else.
Shashwati	: Do you suspect anyone out of these people?
Parikshita	: No, I don't think anyone belongs to that category.
Sandeep	: Dad! Let's assume that a ruffian has planned to take revenge on somebody, and unfortunately you resemble that person. In that case…
Parikshita	: In that case, what?
Sandeep	: Then, that ruffian, probably mistaking you for someone else, might have followed you to identify our house and slipped in that threatening letter.
Shashwati	: Yes, that could be a possibility.
Parikshita	: (Takes a long breath) Yes, that is possible. But I don't remember anyone following me. (The doorbell rings again)
Parikshita	: (Scared) Sandeep!
Sandeep	: What's it, Dad?
Parikshita	: He has come now. There is no escape.
Shashwati	: (Sobbing) Oh, mother! What do we do now?
Sandeep	: Dad! Ask him who is there?
Parikshita	: There's no need to ask. This time, it's definitely him with a sword, dagger, or axe in hand. Shashwati, take Sandeep and go to that room. Give me the vegetable chopper. I will cut off one of his body parts before he tries to behead me.
Shashwati	: (Pulls Parikshita from his backside) No, don't open the door.

Parikshita	: Leave me. Take the children and go to the other room.
Shashwati	: (Leans on the door and tries to overhear) I can hear the sound of quite a few footsteps outside.
Sandeep	: Dad, first you ask them who they are!
Parikshita	: What's the point in asking their names? Let's just call them Kalia, Balia, or Subala. We don't know them, and they won't reveal their real identities. They use fake names and come in disguise. These goons always have eight to ten different aliases.
Shashwati	: Even then, go ahead and ask.
Parikshita	: (Gulping his saliva) Who...who are you all? (Voice from outside- 'We all are your neighbours. Please open the door, Parikshita Babu.')
Shashwati	: I hope they are not pretending to be our neighbours.
Sandeep	: No, this is Nabin Uncle's voice. Dad, you can open the door!
Parikshita	: Let me open the door then. [Voice from outside-'Parikshita Babu! Open the door. We are waiting outside.']
Shashwati	: Why don't you open the door? [Parikshita Babu opens the door. Nabin, Dilip, and Prashant enter the room. They are neighbours of Parikshita Babu.]
Nabin	: What's the matter, Parikshita Babu? You look so scared.
Dilip	: Did the thieves break into your home last night?
Parikshita	: No.
Prashant	: Then, is this about the death of any of your

close relatives? Why do you all look so sad and distressed?

(Parikshita looks at Shashwati and Sandeep. They are in a dilemma about whether it's wise to reveal the truth to the neighbours or not.)

Nabin : What's the matter, Parikshita Babu?

Parikshita : No, it's nothing.

Dilip : What's this 'nothing'? There is something for sure. No one can hide the truth.

Parikshita : No, nothing has happened.

Dilip : Listen to me, Parikshita Babu. Our buildings are right next to each other, so we could hear the chaos and commotion from your house since early morning. My wife told me that your house was robbed by thieves. They threatened you with pistols and knives and took all your belongings.

Nabin : And my house is the closest to yours from the other side. This morning, my wife got up early to pluck flowers and overheard the commotion at your place. She clung to me in fear and was trembling for quite some time.

Prashant : Dilip Babu and Nabin Babu mentioned that something might be wrong at Parikshita Babu's house. Let's go together and check it out. After all, if we don't help as neighbours, who will?

Nabin : Listen Parikshita Babu, it's not fair to hide the truth from your neighbours.

Dilip : Your problem is in a way our problem too, don't you think so?

Sandeep : Some ruffian has threatened to kill my dad.

Shashwati	: Show them that letter, let them read.
Parikshita	: Have a look.
Nabin	: (Takes the paper) Show me. (Nabin, Dilip, and Prashant read the letter.)
Nabin	: You will be beheaded within seven days.
Dilip	: Who has sent you this letter?
Parikshita	: It was stuck onto our door.
Nabin	: How did you find it?
Parikshita	: Someone rang our doorbell early in the morning. When I opened the door, no one was there, but I found this paper inserted there. (Shashwati leaves the room to make tea.)
Prashant	: Why did the person who inserted the letter rang the doorbell?
Nabin	: It's quite straight forward. He probably did it to ensure no one else found the note before Parikshit Babu. That's why he rang the doorbell to alert him about the note and then left before Parikshit Babu could open the door.
Dilip	: The entire thing seems like a well-thought-out plan.
Nabin	: These kind of plans are made to assassinate important people.
Prashant	: Parikshita Babu! You should file an F.I.R. at the Police Station. Everything will be clear if the police investigates the case.
Dilip	: No, no, Parikshita Babu! Please, don't make that mistake.
Prashant	: Mistake? Is it wrong to inform the police? In my opinion that should be the first thing to do in this critical situation.

Nabin : What can the police do? We will not find anything out of the police inquiry. No one will confess the truth.

Prashant : You mean he shouldn't inform the police then?

Nabin : The police can't harm the goons, even if you catch them yourself and hand them over.
(Shashwati comes with the tea at that time. She keeps the tray on the center table)

Shashwati : Please have tea.
(All of them sip tea.)

Nabin : Parikshita Babu! Are you aware of one incident that had happened in this colony last year?

Parikshita : Which incident?

Nabin : It's about that ruffian who dragged Prafulla Babu from the front building, knocked him down on the road, and kept punching and kicking him nonstop.

Dilip : The residents of this colony watched everything from the road, their rooftops, windows, and boundary walls. Fear clouded their minds, and they shuddered from within.

Nabin : He continued to thrash Prafulla Babu and eventually tossed him onto the road like a punctured ball. The police arrived only as the assailant was leaving on his motorbike. Although he was handcuffed by the police, no one agreed to be a witness despite it happening in broad daylight, so he was released.

Dilip : Our fear and reluctance to bear witness to

	such incidents give these ruffians the courage to hit and stab someone so ruthlessly. We are so timid, just standing there helpless and chicken-hearted.
Nabin	: That's why I keep saying that reporting to the police is pointless. Instead, it might cause us more trouble.
Prashant	: How can it harm us?
Nabin	: Do I also need to explain this to you? If that ruffian comes to know that Parikshita Babu has taken the help of the police, he can harm him in a fit of rage. Now, he has threatened Parikshita Babu only, if he gets angry, he can also think of killing his entire family.
Shashwati	: No, we will not inform the police.
Nabin	: Last year something like this had happened in Kolkata.
Shashwati	: What's the incident?
Nabin	: Someone had threatened to kill the owner of a cloth store, if he didn't pay 10 lakh rupees within four days.
Prashant	: What happened next?
Nabin	: What do you expect to happen? Without paying heed to the death threat, the shop owner informed the police. Armed policemen patrolled around his house and shop. Exactly after four days, at midnight, the ruffian eluded the police and murdered the shop owner along with his wife and only son.
Shashwati	: Oh, my God! Oh, My Lord Jagannatha! You are my only savior.
Nabin	: Okay, Parikshita Babu! I think it is dan-

	gerous to inform the police. What is your opinion?
Shashwati	: Why do you need his opinion? We don't want to inform the police.
Nabin	: Well, Parikshita Babu, do you suspect anyone?
Prashant	: Do you have any rivals, particularly anyone who might be a troublemaker or a goon?
Parikshita	: No.
Nabin	: By any chance, have you ever opposed anyone for any illegal activity or injustice, maybe a few months or years ago?
Parikshita	: No, I haven't… yes, yes, I remember.
Nabin	: What do you remember?
Shashwati	: Have you ever harmed anyone?
Parikshita	: That's an old incident.
Shashwati	: How old?
Parikshita	: Almost three years ago, one afternoon, I was returning home from the office. All the shops in the market were closed, and the road was deserted. A dark-complexioned man with a beard was following a girl on the lonely road. The girl asked me for help.
Nabin	: Was she alone?
Parikshita	: Yes she was alone.
Dilip	: What happened next?
Parikshita	: I had an argument with that man. Fortunately at the same time, a police patrol van moved past us. I called for help and the girl explained every thing to the police officer. The police arrested that man, pushed him inside the van and took him to the police station.

Shashwati	:	Why were you so concerned? What was the need to bring trouble for yourself?
Prashant	:	From this incident, it's clear that he is the one who has threatened you.
Shashwati	:	Yes, I think it is none other than him.
Parikshita	:	But this incident happened three years ago. If that man had to take revenge, why didn't he do it immediately within fifteen days, a month or within a year?
Nabin	:	Why? May be because that person was in jail for a while after that incident. It might have taken three years for him to trace your address after being released from prison.
Dilip	:	It is none other than him.
Nabin	:	Well, Parikshita Babu, can you recognize that fellow if you see him now?
Parikshita	:	Yes, I remember his blurred face. He was a six-foot-tall, dark-complexioned man with a broad chest, big eyes, and a tiger-like, frightening face.
Pradeep	:	Dad! A man of that physique stays near our school. We call him a 'demon'. (Nobody pays attention to Pradeep's words.)
Nabin	:	Parikshita Babu, do you know my brother-in-law, Satia?
Parikshita	:	Which one? Your elder brother-in-law?
Nabin	:	No, no, not him, Satia is the younger one. He has good connections with these local hooligans. He lives in the flat behind our office. If you agree, I can call him. You can go with him to identify that man and we can try to reach a settlement.
Dilip	:	Yes, you are right. We don't want any kind

	of tussle, but an amicable solution. Many significant disputes have been resolved over a cup of tea. This is not a big deal.
Nabin	: Our Satia can handle it effortlessly. First, you go with him to identify that ruffian. I will manage the rest. You don't have to do anything.
Shashwati	: Nabin Babu, please call your brother-in-law. Let's get this identification done today itself. We don't mind paying five to seven thousand rupees if needed. There's no point in dragging this issue and letting it escalate.
Nabin	: Have I denied this? I can only proceed if Parikshita Babu agrees.
Shashwati	: His consent is not required. This all happened because of his immaturity. If he had shown a bit more insight, he wouldn't have argued with that ruffian and we wouldn't be in this mess today. I insist... he must go. You please...
Nabin	: Parikshita Babu! What do you say? Are you ready?
Parikshita	: Okay, then. Call your brother-in-law.
Shashwati	: What 'Okay, then'! Are you doing him a favour?
Parikshita	: I just asked him to call his brother-in-law. What's wrong in my words?
Shashwati	: There is no question of inviting him here. This is a life and death situation that mustn't be ignored. It is our problem, so we have to go to him.
Parikshita	: Ok, then. I will go.
Nabin	: Are you afraid that anything might happen

to you on the road? No, no, don't worry. Nobody can touch you if Satia is with you. I can vouch for that.

Parikshita : No, when you are saying…

Nabin : If you've made up your mind, let's leave right away. Satia won't be available if we delay; he's a busy man. If we catch him at his house, he can take you to the goon's den on his motorbike, and you can try identifying that person there.

Shashwati : Hurry up! Why are you still sitting? Get up and go.

Prashant : Parikshita Babu! There is nothing to fear. Please get up.

Dilip : Please go and identify that goon and come back. Then, we all will sit together and find out a solution. Many important conflicts are resolved like this. It is not a big deal.

Prashant : We have to leave for office now. We will take a break around 1.30 PM, by that time, you must have identified that man. We will have a discussion then.

Nabin : Parikshita Babu! Please come. Let's go.

Parikshita : Okay, let's go. (Gets up)

Shashwati : Be careful.

Nabin : Don't worry about that (affectionately). I am telling you, "Nobody will dare to touch Parikshita Babu when our Satia is with him." (Parikshita Babu leaves with Nabin, Dilip, and Prashant. Shashwati immediately shuts the door from inside.)

ACT- III

[At Parikshita's place, an astrologer is sitting on the ground, studying the geometrical lines drawn on the floor. Shashwati and her younger son, Pradeep are sitting close to him.]

Astrologer : (Draws lines on the floor) Come here, daughter! Come close. Take this chalkstone. Place it anywhere inside the circle you wish. (Shashwati looks around and goes to the astrologer with hesitant steps)

Shashwati : He is my younger son, Pradeep. Is it fine if he puts the chalkstone instead of me?

Astrologer : No, that won't work. It should be done by the head of the family.

Shashwati : My husband is not at home. If you can wait for an hour, he will be here.

Astrologer : I can't wait for so long. Daughter! You are now the head of the family in your husband's absence. So keep the chalkstone anywhere in this circle you wish.
(Shashwati holds the chalkstone, examines the circle. Then, she places it at one place.)

Astrologer : All right. Tell the name of a flower now.

Shashwati : Rose.

Astrologer : (He counts the lines of fingers on his hand) Rose. Tell me a fruit's name now.
Shashwati : (Thinks for a while.)
Pradeep : Mango.
Shashwati : Yes, Mango.
Astrologer : No, this won't work. You need to tell me the name of a fruit yourself.
Shashwati : (She thinks again.)
Astrologer : You don't have to think that hard. Spell out whatever name comes to your mind. The name that comes out spontaneously will be the right one.
Shashwati : Coconut.
Astrologer : Tell me a river's name.
Shashwati : Kharsuan river.
Astrologer : (Holding the chalk stone, he draws lines on the floor and counts the lines on his fingers.) You haven't had any connection with your native village for a long time.
Shashwati : No, we don't have.
Astrologer : You also don't have a cordial relationship with the people from your village who live in Bhubaneswar.
Shashwati : You are talking about my village or my husband's village?
Astrologer : Your husband's village.
Shashwati : No, our relationship with them is not bad.
Astrologer : I am not saying that the relationship is strained, but the reading says it is not that cordial. All right, leave that. What's Parikshita Babu's zodiac sign?
Shashwati : Cancer.

Astrologer	:	It's not an auspicious time for this zodiac.
Shashwati	:	Oh, mother! What do I do? Please work it out and let me know what all can be done for prevention.
Astrologer	:	We must appease the planets. Do you have his horoscope with you?
Shashwati	:	Yes, we have.
Astrologer	:	Get that horoscope. Let me calculate for once and all and find out a remedy.
Shashwati	:	Please be seated for a while. I will bring it soon. (Exits)
Astrologer	:	Pradeep Babu! Which class are you in?
Pradeep	:	Class V.
Astrologer	:	Where is your father?
Pradeep	:	He has gone to meet the goons.
Astrologer	:	(Gets startled) Goons? Is your father a goon?
Pradeep	:	No.
Astrologer	:	Then, why has he gone to meet them?
Pradeep	:	Someone has threatened my father to behead him within seven days. He has gone to enquire about the ruffian who might have done that.
Shashwati	:	(Enters) Please take this! (She hands over the horoscope. He studies it and draws some lines on the floor.)
Shashwati	:	Pradeep, you are a small kid. Why are you sitting here with us? Go inside and read your books. (Pradeep leaves hesitantly.)
Astrologer	:	There is a threat to your family. Parikshita Babu's life is in danger.
Shashwati	:	(In tears) What kind of danger, Sir?
Astrologer	:	He is forty-five years, two months, eight

	days old by today. There is a misfortune awaiting him within the next seven days.
Shashwati	: What's that misfortune?
Astrologer	: The reading says within these seven days…
Shashwati	: (Gets terrified) within seven days?
Astrologer	: He may be attacked by a weapon. The enemy is very powerful.
Shashwati	: (Touches the feet of the astrologer) Please save me from this danger, Sir. Please save my husband's life.
Astrologer	: Hold on, daughter. You won't achieve anything by being so impatient. I will arrange for the remedy.
Shashwati	: I am ready to do whatever you say. Please protect the bangles in my hand and the vermilion on my forehead. Please tell me what we must do.
Astrologer	: You have to perform a Yajna in the Shiva Temple for seven days. On the final day you have to feed fifty Brahmins and pay donations. You will also have to keep fast for seven days and give a donation of minimum 10 grams of gold. Will you be able to do all this?
Shashwati	: (Weeps) Yes, I will do it all, Sir. I will perform everything in detail.
Astrologer	: If you do all this, Lord Shiva will be pleased. Once he is pleased, no one will dare to harm you. The other name of Lord Shiva is Ashutosh. He takes the least time to be gratified and blesses people with boons.
Shashwati	: If I do all this, will there be no risk to my husband's life?

Astrologer	:	You be fearless, daughter! Nobody can harm your husband. Okay, give me my fees, daughter!
Shashwati	:	(Hands over to him a hundred rupee note) Please take it, Sir.
Astrologer	:	No, it's not enough. Pay me Five hundred rupees at least.
Shashwati	:	Five hundred rupees?
Astrologer	:	I showed you a way to save a life worth fifty crore rupees. And you are hesitant to pay only five hundred rupees to me? This is not fair.
Shashwati	:	I have only Fifty rupees more with me. Please manage with this.
Astrologer	:	No, my daughter, this is not enough. Only one hundred and fifty rupees for such an important remedy! And that too for you! No, this doesn't seem right.
Shashwati	:	I don't have any more with me now. If you can wait for a while, my husband will come and pay you some more.
Astrologer	:	(Tensed) No, I can't wait here anymore. Today, I have to read horoscopes at two more places.
Shashwati	:	Please wait for only half an hour, sir.
Astrologer	:	(Looks at the watch) No it's late. I can't wait for a moment.
Shashwati	:	Okay then, you may leave today, I will pay you the rest the day you come to appease the planets.
Astrologer	:	(He touches the money on his forehead.) Fine. (Exits)

SCENE- IV

[The scene is set at Parikshit Babu's place in the evening. Dilip Babu, Nabin Babu, and Parikshita Babu are engaged in a discussion.]

Nabin	:	Parikshita Babu, were you able to identify anyone at the goons' den?
Parikshita	:	No.
Dilip	:	Did you go to all the dens that exist in Bhubaneswar?
Nabin	:	When Satia was there to accompany him, he must have taken him to all the possible places. How many places did you visit?
Parikshita	:	Only four places.
Prashant	:	Did you get a close look at the goon?
Parikshita	:	Yes.
Dilip	:	You seem worried. Maybe seeing all those goons together has frightened you.
Parikshita	:	Why only me, anyone who sees them will panic. These ruffians are wandering freely in the broad day light. They fear none, they don't care about anybody.
Nabin	:	If you had identified that man, we could have settled the matter. What should we do next?
Dilip	:	Did you not find any resemblance between

	that man you had encountered earlier and any of the goons you met now?
Parikshita	: No.
Prashant	: In that case, what should be done now?
Parikshita	: I can't decide what to do at this critical moment.
Dilip	: You can do one thing.
Parikshita	: What's that?
Dilip	: Please go to your village for some days along with your family. If someone asks us about you, we will not disclose anything. If you go to your village, that ruffian will not be able to trace you.
Nabin	: Yes, that sounds safe. What do you say Prashant Babu?
Prashant	: It's an excellent suggestion.
Dilip	: You stay at your village for at least two to three months. And then, through liaison change your government quarter to some other unit. That man will never be able to track you down.
Nabin	: We can't challenge these goons and live peacefully at the same time. Today, he has threatened you to behead you. If tomorrow, he does the same to your entire family, then?
Parikshita	: (Gulps his saliva and feels terrified) You are right. But...
Dilip	: Why is this 'but', Parikshita Babu?
Nabin	: You leave for your village today only.
Parikshita	: Today itself?
Nabin	: Who can guarantee that fellow won't come today? Dilip Babu and Prashant Babu, let's go. Let him pack his belongings.

Prashant	: Listen Parikshita Babu, only courage and patience can help you get out of this adverse situation. We are leaving now. Please inform us in case of any emergency.
Nabin	: Please don't hesitate Parikshit Babu! We are your neighbours. If we don't help you at this critical moment then who else will? Now we must leave.
	(The neighbours leave. Parikshita Babu shuts the door. Shashwati and Sandeep enter.)
Sandeep	: Let's not worry about what they say, Dad. Let's go to the police station and file an F.I.R.
Shashwati	: No, there is no need to inform the police. If that man gets angry, he may hold a grudge against my children. We will do what Nabin Babu and others adviced us. Let's go to our village.
Parikshita	: How could you suggest that, knowing every thing? Our neighbors have no idea about our situation in the village. Do we even have a house there? It's completely dilapidated after my parents' death.
Shashwati	: Is it not possible to repair that house?
Parikshita	: It is easier said than done. Our house has been in ruins for two years. The earthen walls have collapsed due to heavy rain. The thatched roof has neither bamboo nor straw left. Repairing it won't work; we need to build a new house. Do you have any idea about the time and money required to build a new house?
Pradeep	: (Enters) Dad, we will build a beautiful new thatched house in the village again and live there.

Parikshita	:	Do you know how much time and money will be spent constructing a house there?
Shashwati	:	If going to the village is not an option now, then what do we do?
Parikshita	:	Let me think for a while. I can't decide anything right now.
Sandeep	:	You are not alone, Dad! Fear can cloud any one's judgment. We should inform the police. At this crucial moment, it would be wise for us to seek their help.
Parikshita	:	Don't even mention their name to me. We won't gain any thing there.
Sandeep	:	Why? Just because these neighbours frightened you. I know them very well. These government employees are intimidated all the time. They are scared of telling the truth, scared of helping anyone, scared of thieves and ruffians and even scared of the police. They lack courage. They didn't come here to help us or build our confidence, they came here to scare us.
Shashwati	:	Lower your voice, they might hear you.
Sandeep	:	Let them hear… I am not afraid of anybody here. The neighbours in this city rarely help each other. They prioritize their safety and security over everything else. That's why they have advised us to go to the village. They think, if we leave, they all will be out of danger. Neither will the police come here nor will they have to go through the questioning by the police. That ruffian won't visit this place and our neighbours will stay safe.

Parikshita	: Nobody helps you in cities. They are all hypocrites. They all pretend to help others. Here, they will witness everything, but if you ask them, they will never admit that they have seen anything. They will say, "We were not present at the spot of the incident."
Sandeep	: If we inform the police, they will send a patrolling team to watch over our quarters.
Parikshita	: How long can they guard our house?
Sandeep	: For seven days.
Parikshita	: If that man comes after seven days when the police cordon is off, then?
Sandeep	: He has warned that he will come within seven days.
Parikshita	: That's true, but if he comes to know about the police cordon, he will wait until the police to leave.
Sandeep	: So, there is no certainty that he will come only within these seven days.
Parikshita	: What kind of certainty you are talking about? Since he has threatened me, he will definitely come within these seven days if there is no police to guard us. Even if there is police patrolling, we can't predict when he might come to assault us. The fear of him will always remain until he appears.
Shashwati	: No, don't get into the police matters. Please listen to me. We can do one more thing.
Parikshita	: What?
Shashwati	: An astrologer had come to our house today in the morning.
Parikshita	: Today? What time?

Shashwati	:	The time you visited the goons' place with Nabin Babu's brother-in-law.
Parikshita	:	What did the astrologer say?
Shashwati	:	He rolled the chalk stone and studied your horoscope. And accurately predicted about the danger hovering over you for these seven days.
Parikshita	:	Really?
Shashwati	:	He is a seer. He said that within seven days your husband…
Parikshita	:	…is probably going to die.
Shashwati	:	Yes, he almost said that. A weapon will be used to assault you.
Parikshita	:	What about the remedies?
Shashwati	:	"We must arrange a Yajna for seven days at the Shiva Temple. On the final day we have to feed fifty Brahmins and offer donations. We also have to donate minimum ten grams of gold."
Sandeep	:	All these are nonsense. He is a fraud.
Shashwati	:	He predicted everything accurately. How can you say he is a fraud?
Sandeep	:	Let me explain it to you. How much did you pay him?
Shashwati	:	He asked for Five hundred rupees, but I paid him a hundred and fifty rupees.
Parikshita	:	He has deceived you off a hundred and fifty rupees. How can you say that he is not a swindler? Have you estimated the amount of expenditure he has proposed for the remedies?
Shashwati	:	Is money more valuable than life?
Parikshita	:	Will I be alive if I perform the yajna for

	seven days at the Shiva Temple? That ruffian will behead me in one blow if he finds me roaming around in open space.
Shashwati	: Don't speak such unfortunate words!
Sandeep	: Let me call all my friends to watch over you at home. That wicked guy won't even dare to come.
Parikshita	: How long will they stay at our house? We can't keep them forever.
Shashwati	: Then, what else can you do?
Parikshita	: In this city life, there is no one to save you but yourself. I have decided not to step out of this house for seven days. I will take leave from work, arm myself with weapons and stay alert. Then, rest is my destiny.
Shashwati	: Is there a weapon in our house to arm yourself with? We live unarmed in this city. We don't even have a single dagger, knife, or even a staff.
Parikshita	: Today, we will buy a long dagger, a sword and at least two staffs from the market.
Sandeep	: And a small axe, too, Dad!
Parikshita	: Yes, you are right. A small axe is the right kind of weapon to assault the enemy from a distance.
Pradeep	: Get me a gun, Dad!
Sandeep	: What will you do with that gun?
Pradeep	: I will shoot that ruffian.
Parikshita	: Pradeep, go and call Nabin uncle.
Shashwati	: Why do you need to call him again?
Sandeep	: You've met all our neighbours in the building. How is Nabin uncle alone going to help you?

Parikshita	:	I will send the leave application to my office through him and ask him to get the weapons from the market.
Sandeep	:	Give me the money. I will buy those weapons from the market and also go to your office to drop the leave application for tomorrow.
Parikshita	:	If you go to the market, that man may…
Sandeep	:	He won't come today.
Parikshita	:	How do you know that?
Sandeep	:	Had he any plans to murder you today, he would not have sent the letter first.
Parikshita	:	No, you ask Nabin Babu to buy the weapons for us.
Sandeep	:	Nabin uncle, Dilip uncle or Prashant uncle, nobody will agree to buy weapons for us.
Shashwati	:	Why?
Sandeep	:	They all will prioritize their safety and security first. They all will come under the threat of that man if they help us.
Parikshita	:	Okay then, you go to the market and buy the weapons.
Shashwati	:	Be careful and vigilant.
Parikshita	:	It won't be right for you to take the 'leave application'. I will send that to office through Nabin Babu.
Sandeep	:	Fine, give me money.
Parikshita	:	(Takes out money from the table-drawer) Take one thousand rupees. Try to manage within that.
Shashwati	:	Watch your step. (Sandeep leaves and Parikshita shuts the door from inside)

SCENE -V

[The location is Parikshita Babu's drawing room. Two staffs, a small axe, and a dagger stand at one corner of the room. Parikshita carefully takes out the weapons one by one, observes the sharpened edges and practices how to use them.]

Shashwati	:	(Watches Parikshita holding all the weapons in his hands) Are you going to stand like this with the staff, axe and dagger in hand?
Parikshita	:	What else I can do?
Shashwati	:	Put them against the wall there. Use them only in need.
Parikshita	:	We don't know when we might need them. That man may reach here at any moment.
Shashwati	:	For how long will you stand holding all those weapons? Please keep them there.
Parikshita	:	Ok, I will keep them aside. But I am feeling very scared.
Shashwati	:	Keep holding the axe. Place the staff and dagger against the wall. I will hand them over to you when you need them.
Parikshita	:	Okay then, I am keeping them here. Hand me over the file that's kept on the center table.
Shashwati	:	Why do you need that?

Parikshita	:	I will tell you. Give it to me first.
Shashwati	:	Take this.
Parikshita	:	(Opens the file) Look, this is my Group Insurance certificate. If I die, you will receive five lakh rupees from the government.
Shashwati	:	Why do you always say such inauspicious words?
Parikshita	:	Death is so unpredictable. It comes suddenly and snatches your life away. You never get time to prepare. But in my case, death has given me a seven-day notice. I will prepare myself within this time frame. Hold this savings certificate. After six months, you will receive two lakh rupees. These are all our legal documents for our land and house in the village.
Shashwati	:	Keep all these with you. No one is going to steal them from our house.
Parikshita	:	You need to understand the complexity of these legal papers. There are many other matters I need to discuss with you. Sandeep's mom, please listen to me.
Shashwati	:	Why are you acting crazy?
Parikshita	:	After my death, you will receive a gratuity and earn family pension from the government. Sandeep will also get a job. And look at this note, the details of my debts and all the money that I have lent to people are mentioned here. Take this, hold it.
Shashwati	:	Are you out of your mind? Why are you blabbering like this?
Parikshita	:	How can someone be in senses when the sword of death is hanging over his head?

Shashwati	:	Your weird behavior is making me anxious. Oh, Mother Goddess! You are our hope and saviour. I will sacrifice a goat to you. Please save us from this danger. Oh, Lord Lingaraj! Save our family. I will shower upon you one lakh Bel leaves. Oh, Lord Jagannath! Hey Chakadola! Once you had fought for this country riding a black horse. Today, you come riding the same black horse my Lord, and save us from this threat.
Pradeep	:	(Enters) Mom, I will go to school today.
Shashwati	:	Pradeep wants to go to school today. What do you say?
Parikshita	:	No, nobody will leave the house for the next seven days. No office for me, no college for Sandeep, no school for Pradeep. We will neither go out nor will anyone come to our home during these seven days.
Pradeep	:	What about the milkman and the newspaper hawker?
Parikshita	:	They will deliver us through the window.
Pradeep	:	How will the milkman deliver through the window?
Parikshita	:	Then, we won't buy milk for seven days.
Sandeep	:	(Enters, holding the dagger.) I will use this.
Shashwati	:	No, no... you don't join this heinous crime and violence.
Sandeep	:	No, I will hold this dagger.
Parikshita	:	Your mom is right. That man has threatened me. Both of us will have a fight. Either he will kill me or I will kill him. You don't interfere in this. If anything happens to you, who will take care of our family?

Pradeep	:	Then, give me that axe. I will strike his neck with a strong blow when he is engaged in a fight with you.
Parikshita	:	You are still a kid. You shouldn't involve yourself in crime.
Shashwati	:	Don't dwell on thoughts of violence all the time. Chant the name of God, the Almighty. Light a lamp and incense sticks before the deity. Express your respect and gratitude to God. If He wills, He will protect us from this great peril. Go to that room. I have arranged flowers, sandal paste, incense sticks, and lamps for worship there. Let's all go and pray together.
Parikshita	:	Please bring Lord Jagannath's photo to this room and hang it on this wall. I will stand here near the door and keep looking into His eyes constantly. I will keep chanting his name in my heart all the time.
Shashwati	:	Please go to that room first. I have arranged the images of Lord Jagannath, Lord Lingaraj, Lord Akhandalmani, Goddess Tarini, Goddess Charchika, and Goddess Mangala there. We will bring Lord Jagannath's photo to this room after the prayer.
Parikshita	:	Then, let's go. [Parikshita gets up holding the small axe and the dagger.]
Shashwati	:	Pradeep and Sandeep. Both of you also come... we all will pray together.

SCENE- VI

[It's night. Parikshita is sleeping. He has kept a dagger, a small axe, and a staff at his bed side. He dreams in sleep. Shashwati is sleeping close to him. The dream scene starts. The doorbell rings in his dream.]

Parikshita : (Shouts loudly) He…is here…he has come. Sandeep's mom! He is here.
[Shashwati wakes up yawning and stretching. The dream scene ends. Parikshita howls from his bed, "He has come… he has come." Shashwati gets up and shakes Parikshita's shoulder to wake him up from sleep.]
Shashwati : What happened? Who has come?
Parikshita : He is here…he is here.
(Parikshita clasps Shashwati, gets up from bed trembling.)
Parikshita : He has come.
Shashwati : Stop it, why are you behaving like this? Who has come? Where is he?
Parikshita : It's that ruffian. He has a big moustache, large eyes, a fierce face like a tiger, and a pitch dark complexion.
Shashwati : Where is he? How did he enter?
Parikshita : He broke open the door.
Shashwati : All the doors and windows are closed and

	intact. Nobody has entered. It is almost midnight. Everybody is sleeping. You also go back to sleep.
Parikshita	: Did you hear the doorbell ring?
Shashwati	: No, I didn't hear anything. Who rang the doorbell and when?
Parikshita	: Didn't you hand me over the dagger then?
Shashwati	: Can you see any dagger in your hand? It is there on the bedside. I was in a deep sleep. I don't know any thing about that.
Parikshita	: Sandeep and Pradeep... both were here. Where have they gone?
Shashwati	: They are sleeping peacefully in the other room.
Parikshita	: So, didn't you hear the sound of the main door breaking?
Shashwati	: No, I haven't. Let's go to the door to check.
Parikshita	: Let's go. [Both of them walk up to the door.]
Shashwati	: See, the door is shut from inside.
Parikshita	: Yes, it is closed. Then, how did it happen?
Shashwati	: Perhaps, you were dreaming.
Parikshita	: Was I dreaming? (Rubbing the eyelids)
Shashwati	: Yes, you were dreaming.
Parikshita	: May be…
Shashwati	: If you think of that person day and night, you will get nightmares like this. Okay, let's go to bed now.

(Shashwati forcefully makes him lie down on the bed. She pulls a quilt over him and switches off the lights.)

SCENE- VII

[Parikshita Babu sits holding a small axe and a dagger. Beside him, two staffs are placed leaning against the wall. Dilip Babu sits before him on the sofa.]

Dilip	:	This is not the right thing you have done.
Parikshita	:	I am not in a condition right now to judge what is wrong and what is right.
Dilip	:	You are behaving just like a kid. You are an adult and the head of the family. Stop acting like a mad…
Parikshita	:	Am I mad? So you think I have gone mad?
Dilip	:	Why do you behave like this if you are not mad?
Parikshita	:	Behave like what…?
Dilip	:	(Looks at the axe and dagger) What are all these?
Parikshita	:	Have you not seen them before? This is a small axe and this one is a dagger. I hope you are familiar with a staff.
Dilip	:	So, this is what you gathered from my words? It's like asking a mango lover what a mango-stone is. We belong to the warrior clan. We have daggers, swords, spears, swordsticks, and many other weapons at our village home. Every year during Durga

	Puja, we sharpen these weapons to worship them.
Parikshita	: Then, why did you ask me about them?
Dilip	: What are you going to do with them?
Parikshita	: If some one attacks me, I will do the same to him.
Dilip	: (Laughs loudly) We know very well how strong you are when it comes to assaulting some one. You are not new to us. Have you ever assaulted anybody anywhere?
Parikshita	: It was not required till now, so I had not.
Dilip	: You mean if you need to assault someone today, you will do it. Are you sure?
Parikshita	: Yes, definitely.
Dilip	: It's not easy to kill someone; it takes a lot of courage. If someone comes to harm you, you might panic, close your eyes in fear and drop the weapon. You would start trembling like a malaria patient. So, why didn't you follow our advice?
Parikshita	: What is that I didn't follow?
Dilip	: It could have been the best solution if you had left for your village with your family. Now, you will die and drag all of us into danger.
Parikshita	: I don't have a house in my village. It is in a state of disrepair.
Dilip	: So what? You could have stayed with somebody else in the village.
Parikshita	: Where would I stay with my entire family for so many days?
Dilip	: How can I say? It's your village and you have to decide that yourself. You could have at least stayed in your father-in-law's house.

Shashwati	:	(Enters) What's the matter, Dilip Babu?
Dilip	:	A ruffian had come to our office today.
Parikshita	:	A ruffian? He came to our office?
Shashwati	:	How does he look like?
Dilip	:	He had a pitch-dark complexion and stood nearly six feet tall. His large, wide eyes resembled car headlights. He sported a tiger-like moustache and his face was marked with pockmarks.
Shashwati	:	Oh, my God, Lord Jagannath! You save us!
Parikshita	:	Why did he come to our office?
Dilip	:	He was asking for you.
Parikshita	:	He was asking for me?
Dilip	:	He wanted to know why Parikshit Babu was on leave and when will he join back.
Parikshita	:	What did you say?
Dilip	:	We are not so stupid to reveal your whereabouts to him. We told him that we have no idea about when Parikshita Babu will be returning to the office. We also asked him to let us know if he had any important work with Parikshita Babu, so we could inform him. However, he didn't say anything.
Shashwati	:	What was his name? Where does he live?
Dilip	:	Do you think we didn't ask him? He didn't reveal his name and address. Instead, he just looked at us with wide, wandering eyes. He sat silently near your chair for quite some time.
Parikshita	:	Did he ask for my home address?
Dilip	:	No.
Shashwati	:	I have not seen a stupid like you anywhere. If that man didn't have your address, then

		how could he insert that letter into our door?
Parikshita	:	Yes, you are right. I had forgotten that.
Sandeep	:	(Enters) Mom, what is it again?
Shashwati	:	That man had come to your father's office today.
Sandeep	:	To the office?
Parikshita	:	Dilip Babu saw him today in our office.
Sandeep	:	How did Dilip uncle know that he was the man?
Parikshita	:	A person was searching for me at our office.
Sandeep	:	Somebody must have some important official work with you. That's why he was searching for you.
Shashwati	:	He was pitch-dark, had a huge moustache and big eyes. He looked dangerous.
Sandeep	:	Is every single person with big moustache, big eyes and black-complexion our enemy?
Dilip	:	His pant-pocket appeared raised as if he had hidden a pistol inside and one of his hands was always in his pocket. His actions seemed suspicious. Our colleagues advised us to inform Parikshita Babu to leave Bhubaneswar and go to his native village.
Sandeep	:	And If we don't leave, then…
Dilip	:	In that case, the next time he comes to the office and asks about Parikshita Babu, then…
Sandeep	:	There are so many people in the office can't some one just call the police to arrest him?
Parikshita	:	Yes, you are right, that sounds sensible.
Dilip	:	What is sensible?
Parikshita	:	If the next time he comes to the office and asks about me, just be cordial with him and make him sit on the chair next to mine.

Sandeep	: To convince him further, spend ten rupees and offer him a cup of tea. Ask him to be seated for a while and you send the peon to fetch Parikshita Babu.
Shashwati	: What nonsense are you saying? If you make that person wait for your father and bring your father there, will that man spare him?
Parikshita	: You just shut up. Nobody meant that.
Shashwati	: Then, why don't you explain what you mean to say?
Parikshita	: Women don't have the brain to understand this kind of schemes and conspiracies. You leave now to the other room. Come back after we finish our discussion.
Shashwati	: Hold on, what do you mean by that? I know how intelligent you are. This problem is the result of your foolishness only. Even after all this, you have the guts to call me brainless?
Sandeep	: Uncle! Give a call to the police station from your office, when the man is busy sipping tea.
Parikshita	: The police will come, arrest that man, and put him in jail. I will return to the office once I know he is behind bars. As long as he is in jail, I will feel safe. Can't you do this small favour for me as a neighbour and well-wisher?
Dilip	: I think you are misleading me.
Parikshita	: Why do you think so? This is the safest way. One phone call, that's all. The police will come and take him into their custody.
Dilip	: And then, once that man is released from jail, he will behead both of us. He won't need to write two letters; he will write one, make

	a photocopy and place it in both our doors. You are the one trembling with fear now and in that case, you will drag me to the gates of Yamapur as well.
Shashwati	: You have already ruined your family. Why do you advise him to destroy his family too?
Dilip	: A drowning man will grab hold of anyone he finds to save his life. Will he ever realize that this will cause both of them to sink to their deaths?
Shashwati	: One's mind gets baffled in adversity. His brain is out of function now.
Sandeep	: Uncle, can you do one more thing?
Dilip	: What?
Sandeep	: It's nothing sort of a tough task. Very easy.
Dilip	: Tell me.
Sandeep	: When that man gets out of the office, you can try to follow him to know where he goes and what is he up to.
Parikshita	: You also can find out how many more people are with him in his team and where he lives.
Sandeep	: If I get this much information, I will have him arrested by the police. He will rot in jail.
Dilip	: I neither need to do anything nor say anything. Whatever you want to do, do it yourself or let your father handle it. I am leaving. (He leaves the spot immediately)
Parikshita	: Dilip Babu! Dilip Babu! Please listen to me.
Shashwati	: What more is there to hear? He has listened to you enough. He has nothing to do with it. Go and shut the door tightly. Don't just stand there.

(Parikshita gets up and shuts the door from inside)

SCENE- VIII

[Sandeep and Pradeep sit in Parikshita Babu's drawing-room. It is the morning of the fourth day. Both of them are sick and tired of staying in their confined room since the last four days.]

Sandeep : It's only one person's fault, but every body are in the jail.
Pradeep : Who is at fault and who is in the jail?
Sandeep : Dad was the one who had an argument with that ruffian years ago. And it's not just Dad; you, me, and Mom are all suffering by shutting ourselves inside this house. Isn't it a jail in itself? We haven't seen daylight for the last four days or gone to the playground. No, enough is enough. I have a cricket match today and I am definitely going.
Pradeep : Cricket match?
Sandeep : Yes, cricket match. Why are you so surprised by this?
Pradeep : I have never seen you play cricket.
Sandeep : You are too young to talk big. How old are you? What do you know about this world? Have you ever seen a cricket match at our Paramount Club?
Pradeep : Where's that?

Sandeep	:	You have yet to learn about the Paramount Club in a small city like Bhubaneswar. What will happen to you when you grow up? You will get lost in metro cities like Delhi, Mumbai and Chennai. Now, leave it. I am heading to the club. Tell Mom,I will return home by noon.
Pradeep	:	I can't tell her. You inform either Dad or Mom before leaving.
Sandeep	:	I don't bother whether you inform them or not, I am leaving. (Looks at the door)
Pradeep	:	Go, if you can. The door is locked.
Sandeep	:	Check where the door key is.
Pradeep	:	You find out. I can't.
Sandeep	:	Pradeep you are a good boy. If I find the key, I will release you first from this jail..Then only I will leave. Let's search for it.Ready one, two , three start..
Pradeep	:	Start.

(Sandeep and Pradeep start searching for the key all over the room—the lower shelf of the centre table, under the mattress, in different shelves, inside the shoes, inside various books and in the almirah. They hear a creaky sound when they search behind a framed image of God hung on the wall. Hearing the sound, Shashwati comes from another room. Sandeep and Pradeep quickly fetch two books and pretend to read like innocent boys.)

Shashwati	:	(Suddenly Shashwati enters) What happened? What's that sound? Pradeep, did you hear any sound?
Pradeep	:	No. (Nods his head for a no.)
Shashwati	:	I heard the sound. It was loud. Both of you

	are sitting in this room, so how both of you didn't hear anything?
Sandeep	: No, Mom, we were engrossed in reading. We did not pay any attention to that.
Pradeep	: Yes, mom! I agree with Sandeep Bhai.
Shashwati	: You were so preoccupied with your studies that you couldn't hear such a loud sound?
Sandeep	: Reading is a kind of addiction, Mom! You know, there was a scientist who was so engrossed in solving a math problem that he didn't even realize a war had started around him. The sound of guns and cannons was inaudible to him.
Pradeep	: Is this true, Sandeep Bhai?
Sandeep	: Do you think I am lying to my Mom?
Pradeep	: Was he killed in the battle?
Sandeep	: If you don't believe me, why don't you ask your teacher?
Pradeep	: Why don't you tell me what happened to that scientist finally?
Sandeep	: Go and ask your teacher.
Shashwati	: If that sound didn't come from inside the house, then did it come from outside?
Sandeep	: You unlock the door. Let me go out and check.
Shashwati	: You want to go outside? No, dear no. if that man sees you, he will behead... (Bites her tongue in guilt), I should not utter such inauspicious words. Both of you sit there and continue with your reading. (Shashwati goes inside again.)
Sandeep	: How can we study at this critical moment? The terror of the swords, axes, and knives

	does not allow us to go outside and again the sight of these weapons inside the house scare the life out of us. (Gives a look at the weapons leaning against the wall) In this situation books also will get scared, tuck their tails and run away.
Pradeep	: We have no other way to escape from this room. Well, Bhai, is it possible for Dad to fight all alone against that man with these weapons?
Sandeep	: Are you a fool? Do you think our Dad has ten hands like Goddess Durga? How can he wield so many weapons at a time? He can hold only one.
Pradeep	: Then, why are so many weapons here?
Sandeep	: I will wield one.
Pradeep	: You will hold one. Then, what about the other weapons? I must have one.
Sandeep	: You are too small to wield a weapon. You can't even lift a single one.
Pradeep	: Stop boasting. Why can't I? I can lift two weapons with both my hands at the same time.
Sandeep	: Let's see, try lifting one.
Pradeep	: Can I try?
Sandeep	: Do it.
	(Pradeep goes to the place where the weapons are. He holds the small axe first. Looks around, and lifts that.)
Pradeep	: Yes, I can lift.
Sandeep	: Why do you show off as if you have raised a mountain? That's just a small axe. Can you

	wave that axe? Show me a demo on how to fight the enemy with that.
Pradeep	: If Dad or Mom comes in, then?
Sandeep	: I am keeping a watch, you try to swing it. I will alert you if any one of them comes in.
Pradeep	: No, if Dad comes to know, he will thrash me.
Sandeep	: You know you don't have the strength to wave that axe. Why are you lying?
Pradeep	: Who says I can't? I will show you.
Sandeep	: Yes, show me. (Pradeep starts waving the small axe standing in the middle of the room. After two to three rounds, it slips away from his hands and falls on the floor. Just then, Parikshita enters from another room. That axe falls right before him.)
Parikshita	: (Gets angry) What's going on? You stupid! Are you not too small to play with an axe? (Pradeep stands there shivering with fear. Parikshita makes him sit on the sofa, and twists his ears in disgust.)
Parikshita	: Is this the way you study? (To Sandeep) You are grown up. Can't you stop him?
Pradeep	: (Starts weeping) It's not my fault, Dad! Bhai told me to do that.
Sandeep	: Shut up! I will give you one tight slap. Why are you blaming me? You were the one hankering after that axe, don't accuse me now.
Pradeep	: Did you not tell me?
Sandeep	: It was you, not me. You only asked, "How can Dad hold all these weapons. I will hold one."

Parikshita	:	Stop arguing. Get your books and read here silently. Are you going? (Sandeep and Pradeep start reading the books in their hands. Parikshita brings that axe and places it against the wall. He kneels down to pay homage to the weapons. He touches the edges of the weapons to examine their sharpness. Pradeep and Sandeep observe this while reading their books. Meanwhile the doorbell rings.)
Sandeep	:	Dad! The doorbell!
Parikshita	:	Let it ring. (The doorbell rings again. Parikshitais startled as it rings. Shashwati enters from the other room.)
Shashwati	:	Who is at the door?
Parikshita	:	(In fear) He…he… must be that man.
Shashwati	:	What should we do now?
Parikshita	:	I will stop him with this weapon. (Parikshita waves the axe. Sandeep and Pradeep stand near their father holding two more weapons.)
Sandeep	:	I will hold this dagger.
Pradeep	:	I will hold this knife.
Parikshita	:	No, both of you leave this room. You are just kids. I will fight with him. A warrior will fight with another warrior of equal strength (The doorbell rings again at that time)
Shashwati	:	Ask him who is there ringing the bell. Who knows, it might be someone else.
Parikshita	:	No, it's him only this time. Who else will come so early in the morning?
Shashwati	:	Sandeep! You ask who is there.

Sandeep	: Who? Who is ringing the doorbell? (A male voice is heard from outside- Please open the door, Parikshita Bhai! I am Somnath.)
Sandeep	: Mom, who is this Somnath?
Shashwati	: Why are you asking me? Ask him.
Sandeep	: Somnath who?
Somnath	: I have come from Koraput.
Shashwati	: Oh, he is your uncle.
Sandeep	: Uncle?
Shashwati	: He is Prabha's husband, Somnath.
Parikshita	: Are you alone or someone is with you?
Somnath	: No, I have come alone. Open the door. Fast.
Shashwati	: What are you thinking? Open the door.
Parikshita	: But...if...
Shashwati	: Why again 'but'? Give me the key. (Shashwati goes to open the door.)
Parikshita	: No, Shashwati! Don't open the door.
Shashwati	: What happened again?
Parikshita	: I have doubts.
Sandeep	: What kind of doubt?
Shashwati	: I am sure about Somnath's voice. It's him. What do you say?
Parikshita	: These ruffians are good at mimicking other's voices. I can firmly say, He is not Somnath.
Shashwati	: No one can imitate him so accurately. It doesn't look nice to make him wait outside for such a long time. He may think otherwise.
Sandeep	: It's not difficult to imitate somebody's voice. A lot of people are doing the same these days. I have watched someone on the T.V. mimicking all the film stars accurately.
Pradeep	: I have watched that too. He was mimicking

	all of them... Amitabh Bachhan, Salman Khan, Shahrukh Khan, Hrithik Roshan and Akshay Kumar.
Parikshita	: Is it that difficult to imitate our Somnath's voice?
Shashwati	: How can that man imitate him when he doesn't know him?
Parikshita	: How can I say how and why he did it?
Sandeep	: Mom, there is another possibility.
Shashwati	: What?
Sandeep	: Let's assume that fellow has been keeping an eye on our house. When he saw Somnath uncle approaching, he took him at gunpoint and forced him to press the doorbell.
Pradeep	: This kind of incidents happen in Hindi films.
Parikshita	: Yes, that is a probability. (The doorbell rings again.)
Parikshita	: (Startled) No, don't open the door.
Somnath	: Open the door. Why are you taking so much of time?
Parikshita	: You all go to that room. Move fast. (Shashwati, Sandeep, and Pradeep run to the other room. The doorbell rings repeatedly. Parikshita keeps standing like that closing his ears. The stage lights are off.)

LAST SCENE

["It's the morning of the fifth day. A photo of Lord Jagannath hangs on the wall of Parikshita Babu's drawing room. Parikshita's entire family prays before the image with folded hands. Parikshita sings, 'Ahe Nila Shaila Prabal Mattabaran, Mo Arata Nalini Bana ku Kara dalana.'"When the song gets over, they all bend their heads down to touch the ground before Lord Jagannath to pay homage.]

Parikshita	:	Oh, my Lord Jagannath! Chakadola! Baliyarbhuj! You alone can rescue me. Save our family from this danger. Oh, Lord! I have not asked for the police support. I have surrendered myself under the shelter of your feet. Oh,Lord,Patitpaban! If you want to protect me, do it, if you want to kill me, do it.It is your wish.
Shashwati	:	Can you hear me?
Parikshita	:	Tell me.
Shashwati	:	For how long can we confine ourselves in this closed room?
Sandeep	:	It's been five days. I am going mad.
Shashwati	:	We are out of vegetables. For how long can we depend only on Dal and mashed potatoes?
Pradeep	:	I want to go outside to play today, Dad!

Parikshita	: Life is more precious than delicacies, games, and outings. Once we lose this valuable life, it won't come back. Who knows where a person goes after death and what happens next? Do they regain a human life or become a cow, goat, bird, or insect? Or does this life, made of the five elements, disintegrate and dissolve back into those same elements?
Sandeep	: You only should stay confined inside the house because that man has threatened you. What is the problem if I visit my friends for a while?
Pradeep	: Dad, please open the door for a while. I will come back in half an hour.
Parikshita	: It has already been five days, and only two more days are left. We will manage to spend them somehow. Come here, let's stand before Lord Jagannath and gaze into his wide eyes. Time will fly by. (Meanwhile Shashwati shouts, looking at the window curtain.)
Shashwati	: Oh, Mother!
Parikshita	: What happened? What happened?
Shashwati	: (She shivers with fear while pointing towards the window) Look at the window. There is someone's shadow on the curtain.
Sandeep	: Where is that?
Shashwati	: On... that... window. (A shadow of a dagger reflects on the window curtain.)
Parikshita	: He has come... he is here. Shashwati, the God of Death, Yamaraj is here.
Sandeep	: That's the shadow of a dagger.

Shashwati	: Oh, my God! Save us.
Parikshita	: Oh Lord, Jagannath! Only you can rescue us. Spread out your twelve-hand-long sword, my God! Protect us from this danger. Where is my small axe?
Shashwati	: Take this.
Parikshita	: (Waves the axe) Hey, Sandeep! Pradeep! Both of you go to the other room.
Shashwati	: Oh, my God! Save us! Oh, *Chakadola* (Jagannath)! You are omnipresent, you can see everything, Lord! Hey, Maa Cuttack Chandi! Hey, Maa Tarini! Hey, Lord Lingaraj! O, Lord, Save us! Save my husband (She pulls Parikshita towards her.) Please, don't go near the window.
Parikshita	: Oh, you leave me, leave me.
Sandeep	: Why are you behaving crazy, Dad?
Parikshita	: Look, there, the shadow of a dagger on the window curtain. That dagger will behead me. Sandeep! Take your mom and Pradeep to the other room.
Sandeep	: No, Dad! I will hold this dagger and stand here with you.
Shashwati	: Sandeep! Don't involve yourself in violence! Oh, My Goddess! Oh, my God! What should I do now? My legs are trembling like a reed in the wind. Hey, Nabin Babu! Hey, Prashant Babu! Hey, Dilip Babu! Rush to us.
Parikshita	: No, don't call them. City neighbours are good only for parties, weddings and picnics. They act deaf and dumb during critical times. Don't expect them to come.
Shashwati	: Oh, Lord Jagannath! Baliyarbhuj! Protect

Parikshita Awaiting and Siddhartha The Other | 81

	my bangles, Lord! Protect the vermilion on my forehead! I will donate a flag to Puri Srimandir. I will offer you one lakh champa flowers.
Parikshit	: Move, you move from here, Sandeep! Go to that room.
Sandeep	: No, I will be here with you. I will see how he kills you when I am here. I will chop him into two pieces with this dagger.
Parikshita	: He is here to hit me. You all stay away from this. He has a dagger, but I have my axe in my hand. I will behead him before he strikes me. (Parikshita moves towards the window.)
Shashwati	: (She pulls Parikshita from behind.) No, don't go there.
Parikshita	: Leave me, Shashwati! Today, it's either him or me; one of us is surely going to die. Leave me, I'm telling you, leave me!
Shashwati	: Why are you behaving so irrationally? Stay back, don't go there.
Parikshita	: If he enters the house, he will not spare anybody. You all go to that room. I am here. I will strike him hard on his neck if he tries to enter breaking through the window.
Pradeep	: Dad! Dad! Look, Chintu just ran away. Dad, please open the door! Open it fast. Chintu ran away.
Parikshita	: What? Chintu? Who is he? Where did he go? Death is here to take me away by grabbing my hair and for you, it's just a child's play?
Pradeep	: No, Dad! Please open the door. (knocks on the door) Open the door. He is the devil Chintu. I will teach him a lesson.

Shashwati	: Hey, who is Chintu?
Pradeep	: My friend Chintu. He was standing near our window with a dagger in hand. I saw him running away.
Parikshita	: Your friend? Why was he standing there with a dagger? What are you saying? Are you in your senses?
Pradeep	: Yes, Dad! I saw him through the gap of the window curtain. I know it is Chintu. Open the door, Dad!
Sandeep	: Yes Dad! Open the door. The shadow of the dagger is not there anymore.
Parikshita	: No, no. The shadow was that of an adult. It was not of a small child. He is not Chintu. He is that ruffian.
Sandeep	: The shadow gets elongated in the morning sunlight. That's why Chintu's shadow appeared tall. Pradeep is correct. That was Chintu.
Pradeep	: Open the door, Dad!
Shashwati	: Are you sure, that was Chintu?
Pradeep	: Yes, mom. He was Chintu.
Sandeep	: I am opening the door, Dad?
Parikshita	: No, no, don't open. I am too scared. Every thing will be finished if we find that ruffian there instead of Chintu.
Pradeep	: No, Dad! I have seen him with my own eyes. It was none other than Chintu. Open the door, please. (Sandeep opens the door, and Pradeep runs outside.)
Shashwati	: He has gone alone. Sandeep, go follow him! Take this dagger with you.

Sandeep	:	No, mom! No need of the dagger. I will come back soon. (He runs after them.)
Parikshita	:	(He shuts the door from inside.) Oh... in the end, a small kid threatened me? When a man is terrified, everything seems dangerous to him. He sees a needle as a gun, a cat as a tiger and a rope as a snake.
Shashwati	:	I was too scared. God is great. He saved our family.
Parikshita	:	The Almighty has taken this test. He is testing our courage and patience. We have to keep ourselves alert for two more days.
Shashwati	:	Did you shut the door from inside?
Parikshita	:	Yes, why did you ask?
Shashwati	:	Both our children are outside, and you have shut the door. Open it immediately.
Parikshita	:	Yes, you are right. It is a mistake. A man in fear makes so many blunders. (Parikshita opens the door. Pradeep, Sandeep and Chintu enter the room. Chintu holds a dagger in his hand. Pradeep and Sandeep drag him inside.)
Chintu	:	Leave me, I say leave me. Wait for a while, you cheat. I swear, I will chop you into pieces.
Pradeep	:	Don't even dare. If you want to kill me then you should confront me directly. Don't come sneaking like a thief.
Parikshita	:	Hey, what's going on here?
Chintu	:	Uncle! If you truly care about your wellbeing, tell Pradeep to let go of my hand now. Otherwise, don't blame me later.
Sandeep	:	Why are you babbling like that? Shut up and be quiet.

Chintu	: Who are you? This is between Pradeep and me. Once I'm triggered, I won't spare anyone. I'll chop all into pieces.
Shashwati	: Hello, my son! What kind of behavior is this? Are you not Pradeep's friend?
Chintu	: Yes, I am his friend. That doesn't mean that they all will gang up to hit me from all corners.
Parikshita	: Leave him.

(Sandeep and Pradeep release Chintu. Chintu tries to run away from there with his dagger. Parikshita gets hold of him.)

Parikshita	: Hey, hold your patience and remain calm. Why are you mad at us? Let's find out what's the matter and settle it.
Chintu	: No settlement. I will chop Pradeep into pieces for sure. That's all.
Pradeep	: Don't even dare.
Parikshita	: Stop, Pradeep! Shut up and stand quietly.

(Nabin, Dilip, and Prashant enter.)

Parikshita	: Please come in.
Dilip	: Who is this kid with a dagger?
Parikshita	: He is Chintu.
Prashant	: Chintu who?
Sandeep	: He is Pradeep's classmate. He is the son of the driver Nabaghana Rana, who lives near the Maruti Temple.
Nabin	: Why is he holding a dagger?
Parikshita	: I was asking him that question when you all entered. All right, my son Chintu! Why were you standing near our window with a dagger?
Chintu	: I was here to kill Pradeep.

Nabin	:	How dare you? You are such a small kid, and you are here threatening to kill?
Chintu	:	Why not? He has hit me in school. I will not spare him? I will chop him into pieces.
Parikshita	:	When did he hit you? He has not left the house nor gone to the school since the last five days.
Chintu	:	I am not talking about these last five days. He was going to school before that. Wasn't he?
Dilip	:	Why did he hit you?
Chintu	:	Why don't you ask him?
Parikshita	:	Hey Pradeep! Why did you hit him?
Pradeep	:	No, Dad, I never hit him. He is a liar.
Chintu	:	Oh! You seem to be very truthful. I will beat you black and blue until you reveal the truth. Who hit me behind the school?
Pradeep	:	We were wrestling there.
Chintu	:	Didn't you knock me down and punch my nose sitting on my chest while wrestling?
Pradeep	:	You also have wounded my leg by scratching it.
Chintu	:	That was nothing. I would have beheaded you if our teacher had not reached there that moment.
Parikshita	:	Okay, wait...wait...you... (Thinks for while) had come to behead Pradeep. Shashwati! Give me...give me that letter quickly. Why are you looking at me like a fool? Give that letter to me.
Shashwati	:	Which letter?
Parikshit	:	The letter, the one about someone beheading me.

Shashwati	:	What are you going to do with that?
Parikshita	:	Give it to me, fast.
Shashwati	:	(She hands it over to him from the center table.) Here it is.
Parikshita	:	Look, Chintu, look here. Have you written this letter?
Chintu	:	Yes, I have written this. So what? Any problem?
All	:	What! You have written this letter?
Chintu	:	Yes, I wrote this letter.
Pradeep	:	No, Dad! He is lying. I can identify his handwriting. This is not written by him.
Chintu	:	I am not a fool like you to write it myself. I had told one of my friends to write it for me.
Parikshita	:	Hey Chintu! So, you are the one behind this big stunt? Since the last five days I have been waiting for death like king Parikshita in a confined room. Just because I was scared of a small child.
Shashwati	:	He is just a small kid but look at his arrogance! He sends a threatening letter first and then comes with a weapon to kill us?
Chintu	:	Don't advise me, control your son. If he ever touches me again, I will show him the real me. I will slice his hands, legs into nice pieces and separate his head from his body. (Chintu walks some steps, stops and roars.) Hey henpecked, eunuch! I won't harm you today. You are going to come out of the house one day for sure. I will see who will protect you that day. I will ride on your chest and stab you hard, I swear on my mother's grave. (Exits)

Nabin	: Oh, my God! He is a poisonous snake.
Dilip	: Chintu is not the only one; many children these days are like poisonous snakes.
Prashant	: How can we prevent that? They always watch people getting stabbed with knives and daggers, killed by firing and bomb blasts in the middle of the road in broad daylight. They read detailed reports on riots, robberies and rapes in the newspapers. In theaters, movies and television they often watch the dreadful sights of murders, shootouts and violence.
Nabin	: The same children who are so cute, gentle, calm, and docile like Lord Krishna at birth can turn into wild demons under the pressure of circumstances. They are the ones who create chaos and terror everywhere by committing heinous crimes such as murder, rape, kidnapping, and treason.
Parikshita	: Children are the future of our country. We must keep them away from violence if we want to free our country from the clutches of terrorism. Keeping them away from violence is not just the responsibility of their parents, but also yours, mine, and every one's.
Nabin	: Yes, it is every one's responsibility.

(The entire audience comes forward and says, "This responsibility is yours and ours too.")

END

Siddhartha The Other

Dramatist Personae

Siddhartha	:	Son of Rajendra Choudhury
Lopa	:	Fiancée of Sidhartha
Rajendra	:	Father of Siddhartha and an industrialist
Sambit	:	Siddhartha's friend
Kubera	:	God of wealth in the heaven
Agni	:	God of Fire
Vishnu	:	God, the Almighty

SCENE-I

[It's afternoon. Siddhartha and Lopamudra sit together at the edge of a stream. The stream burbles as it travels along its bed, the birds twitter adding serenity to the ambience.]

Lopa : Your negative attitude towards this life, this world and the surroundings is the reason why you can't enjoy your life, Siddhartha!

Siddhartha : The truth can't be denied, Lopa! Not accepting the truth is hypocrisy.

Lopa : Truth is relative Siddharth! Life is above the binary of truth and lie. Enjoy your life. The more time you spend in sorrow, the more you shorten your life.

Siddhartha : But death is the ultimate truth. It is God. It is eternal. Satya, Shiva, Shashwat.

Lopa : Life is both truth and beautiful.

Siddhartha : No, Lopa! Life is a delusion, death is the real truth. Life comes to us in one way, but death in many ways.

Lopa : You are an escapist. Learn to face the reality of life.

Siddhartha : Death is more powerful and influential than life. Death is always there hovering over your life. Man at all times is in shivers with the fear of death. Death, like a lethal weapon

		chases life and life, out of panic, flees away cowardly.
Lopa	:	A person with this kind of attitude will suffer throughout his life. He can't enjoy life, even though wealth and prosperity are at his disposal. The day he steps on this earth, the horror of death will scare the life out of him.
Siddhartha	:	The crude and dangerous figure of death stands in front of all your dreams of a happy and prosperous life. It waves at you with an invitation.
Lopa	:	Give me your hand, Siddhartha! Come close to me. Why are you so indifferent? I am your fiancée. We are the life partners for eternity.
Siddhartha	:	(Silent)
Lopa	:	Why are you silent still, Siddhartha? It is only you and me here in this serene, splendid, solitary natural surroundings. (She giggles) Adam and Eve!
Siddhartha	:	Get back to normal, Lopa! An emotional person can't experience the truth.
Lopa	:	This lush green forest, the gorgeous mountains, the flowing stream and our youth have enchanted me, Siddhartha! This is not the place for exploring the truth. This breath taking ambience is meant for falling in love and enjoy life.
Siddhartha	:	I see a skeleton inside your soft, delicate flesh. I can see the dead body lurking inside every active human life.
Lopa	:	You are very pessimistic, Siddhartha!
Siddhartha	:	I can hear the palpitation of death in the vein of life. A man marches towards death

	in every single step he takes. I can clearly see a queue of human beings moving on the path of death. I can see the falcon of death swooping down on the dove of life every single moment.
Lop	: Please, stop your nonsense, Siddhartha!
Siddhartha	: Life comes with a notice, but death comes accidentally. Nobody knows when will death come and snatch you away in the middle of your meal. There is no certainty of its arrival.
Lopa	: An ascetic mentality has invaded your body.
Siddhartha	: No, Lopa! You are mistaken.
Lopa	: I am not wrong at all. You are totally abstinent from this worldly life, just like the world-famous Siddhartha read in history books. He became an ascetic after seeing an old beggar, a sick person and a corpse. What have you seen…?
Siddhartha	: No; neither have I accepted asceticism nor do I have any desire to go for it.
Lopa	: Siddhartha's lessons say "Desire is the cause of sorrows and suffering." "The end to desire leads to the end of sorrows and brings salvation."
Siddhartha	: But I will say that Siddhartha was hopeful and he also had a desire.
Lopa	: Really? What's that?
Siddhartha	: Salvation was his desire.
Lopa	: Don't you have any desire?
Siddhartha	: Yes, I have.
Lopa	: What's that?
Siddhartha	: He told us that life is full of sorrows and

	plights. He always desired for salvation and wanted freedom from the cycle of life. But I want freedom from the clutch of death. The more dearly I love my life the more afraid I am of death.
Lopa	: Let's go, Siddhartha! Let' run away to a lonely island where you and I will be the only inhabitants. Only you and I. There will be no sorrows. We will enjoy our life to the fullest.
Siddhartha	: But death will be there too. Death is every where, it's there in the lonely island, on the soaring mountain peak, in the endless sky and in the vast ocean. Everywhere, every moment, death is ready for an ambush.
Lopa	: We will enjoy relishing every moment of our life before death touches us. We will cast our offsprings and they will represent us after our death.
Siddhartha	: They will represent us but…they are not us. I want our long life.
Lopa	: You only told me a few minutes before that life is a lie while death is the ultimate truth. How can you talk about a long life now? You want to avoid me with your absurd, impractical story.
Siddhartha	: No, Lopa!
Lopa	: If you love life so much, why do you hesitate to enjoy life? Are you not interested to marry me?
Siddhartha	: You are exceptionally touchy Lopa! I love you very much from the core of my heart. I earnestly want to marry you. But…

Lopa	:	That means your love is conditional with a 'but'.
Siddhartha	:	Try to understand me, Lopa! May be I am not being able to express myself properly.
Lopa	:	Indeed, Siddhartha! I need help understanding you properly. You love me and want to marry me but always try to run away from marriage. You say you love life, but every moment, you shiver at the thought of death.
Siddhartha	:	When life is so uncertain, how will you justify marrying someone and establishing a family? Just assume if I die on the fourth night of our marriage, then?
Lopa	:	Siddhartha!
Siddhartha	:	Every day, these kind of misfortunes happen in the world. It's nothing new.
Lopa	:	It also is a possibility that nothing wrong will happen to you on that fourth night.
Siddhartha	:	If not with me, it may happen to you.
Lopa	:	May be, may not be.
Siddhartha	:	After some years of our marriage you or I shall die. There is also a probability of both of us dying.
Lopa	:	Even that may not happen.
Siddhartha	:	If all these don't happen, then old age will overpower us someday. Our body will weaken, and sensory organs will deteriorate. Step by step we will march towards death every day.
Lopa	:	By that time, we will have lived our life.
Siddhartha	:	No, Lopa! In the world of my dreams, every man or woman will possess an eternal life

and will remain young forever. There will be no fear of death.

Lopa : Will that be possible?

Siddhartha : I will try my best to make it possible.

Lopa : Don't chase after the impossible, Siddhartha! You may lose your life before you complete your research.

Siddhartha : You only branded me as a pessimist just a few minutes ago, but I can see you are a pessimist, not me. I am hopeful that I will be successful in my research. I am leaving on a journey to pursue my research now. (He starts walking.)

Lopa : Wherever you go, please take me along with you. I will go with you.

Siddhartha : No, Lopa! It won't be right for you to go with me. You wait for me. I will certainly return to you one day. (He starts walking again. Lopa follows him.)

Lopamudra : How long will I wait for you, Siddhartha?

Siddhartha : You know very well how difficult this arduous task I am undertaking now is. I am not sure of my return.

Lopa : You still have doubts on your return?

Siddhartha : No, Lopa! I assure you that I will return. Wait for me.

Lopa : But till when? How long will I wait for? By the time you return, my hair probably will have turned grey, my eyes and ears probably will have become dysfunctional. Both of us probably will have grown old.

Siddhartha : No, Lopa! I will return with eternal youth and a long life for you, me, and the entire

		human race.
Lopa	:	Don't run after the impossible and uncertain, Siddhartha! You will suffer; I will, too. Your parents and all your well-wishers will suffer because of you. You will destroy your entire life in doing research only.
Siddhartha	:	The obstacles that stood before the world-famous Siddhartha were his parents, wife, and the entire state. Had he not overcome those adversaries, he would not have achieved the divine knowledge.
Lopa	:	Siddhartha became "Buddha" after attaining enlightenment or divine knowledge and was worshipped worldwide as a great person, but what did his wife Yashodhara gain?
Siddhartha	:	But I will return with a gift of love for you, me and for the humanity.
Lopa	:	Gift? What kind of gift?
Siddhartha	:	Nothing else but eternal youth and long life. Let me move on the untrodden path of my life, Lopa!
Lopa	:	No, don't go, Siddhartha! Don't go.
Siddhartha	:	I will go, Lopa! Bid farewell to me happily. Your heartfelt wishes will help me achieve the attainment. (Leaves)
Lopa	:	(In sadness) Siddhartha!

SCENE-II

[The location is the modern-looking drawing room of industrialist Rajendra Choudhury. Lopa cries out of sorrow and guilt. Rajendra consoles her.]

Rajendra : If you get heartbroken like this, we will be ruined, my daughter! We have to be patient.

Lopa : (sorrowfully in a breaking voice) No, Dad! I am incapable of convincing Siddhartha. I couldn't keep the words I promised you earlier.

Rajendra : You are not at fault, my daughter!

Lopa : Perhaps I am not blessed with the beauty and attributes to attract Siddhartha's mind and soul. I am not suitable to be your daughter-in-law. You had hopes on me …but…

Rajendra : No, Lopa! You are extraordinarily gorgeous and incomparable in beauty and nature.

Lop : But I couldn't change Siddhartha's mind.

Rajendra : Siddhartha's mind is overpowered with the thoughts of 'Death'. He has lost his common sense.

Lopa : But Siddhartha says he loves life the most. He is not ready to sacrifice his life in the hands of death.

Rajendra : This is not a new story. Nobody is ready to accept death.

Lopa	: Siddhartha left to continue his research on a life free of ageing and death.
Rajendra	: He is completely mad now. He will face death if he runs after the impossible.
Lopa	: I heard Siddhartha is visiting various places in the country and searching for an ageless youthful immortal life.
Rajendra	: Siddhartha is very stubborn, my dear! His degree of stubbornness has increased after his mother's death. Still, we must try to stop him from doing this.
Lopa	: He is not ready to listen to anybody. I have tried my best to convince him, but he is firmly stubborn to his words.
Rajendra	: I have sent people to follow him. I have also written letters to all our relatives and Siddhartha's friends. If they find Siddhartha anywhere, they will immediately inform me.
Lopa	: It has been fifteen days since Siddhartha left home. He is visiting different places and interacting with subject experts and intellectuals.
	[Meanwhile the doorbell rings.]
Rajendra	: Who's there? The door is open; please come in.
Sambit	: (Enters) Namaskar, Uncle!
Rajendra	: Come in, Sambit! Be seated. Let me introduce you. He is Sambit, Siddhartha's friend. They were close friends during their post-graduation period. She is Lopa, Siddhartha's fiancée.
Lopa	: Namaskar!
Sambit	: Namaskar!

Rajendra	: I had sent you a letter regarding Siddharth. Did you receive it, Sambit?
Sambit	: Yes, I have. And I have also met Siddhartha after receiving your letter.
Rajendra	: Where is he now? What is he doing?
Lopa	: Have you talked to Siddhartha?
Sambit	: Yes, Siddhartha now continues with the search for heaven.
Rajendra	: The search for heaven? Has he completely gone mad?
Sambit	: No, Uncle! He is physically sound and normal. I have discussed it with him for almost an hour.
Lopa	: Siddhartha had left on a search for an immortal life. But did he change his mind as you said he is seeking for heaven now?
Sambit	: No, Lopa Madam! He has not changed his mind.
Rajendra	: Then, what's this search for the heaven again? Why will he go to heaven?
Lopa	: Is it possible to go to heaven?
Sambit	: He came to know from his research that life in heaven is immortal and youthful for ever, that's why he has decided to go to heaven.
Rajendra	: Mad! Completely mad! Can man ever reach heaven? Have you seen any?
Sambit	: But Siddhartha says a lot of people have gone to heaven alive.
Rajendra	: Those are mythological stories only. This is impossible in this scientific age.
Sambit	: Siddhartha is moving fast towards the Himalayas now-a-days.
Rajendra	: Now only you told us that he is continuing

	with his search for heaven, but then how you are talking of Himalayas at the same time!
Sambit	: I asked Siddhartha the same questin. He told me, "Those who have gone to heaven in the past have been able to do so only through austerity and meditation. The Himalayas are the best place to practice austerity and meditation."
Lopa	: It is impossible now to observe austerity in the Himalayas, it is full of wild and untamed creatures. There is threat to life every moment.
Rajendra	: It may be possible in the day time but not in the night. It's totally impossible to save one's life from the wild beasts even for a single night.
Lopa	: Try to dissuade Siddhartha and save his life from this unfeasible task, Dad! His life is in danger.
Sambit	: I have come here to convey to you that his life is at risk. Keep him away from this impossible task.
Rajendra	: He is very stubborn. Nobody can convince him and divert his thoughts so easily.
Lopa	: But his life is...
Rajendra	: I can understand that very well, daughter! Siddhartha is my only child. No father can keep him cool in this kind of a situation. We have to do something.
Lopa	: Whatever you want to do, do it fast. Otherwise, we will regret later.

Rajendra	: I am ready to do anything for Siddhartha. But I don't know what to do now.
Sambit	: What do you think about deploying security guards around the place Siddhartha sits in meditation?
Rajendra	: Nice idea! I think, that's the only option.
Lopa	: Whatever you want to do, do it immediately, Dad!
Sambit	: Siddhartha is walking to the Himalayas on foot. We must reach the foothills of the Himalayas before he reaches there.
Lopa	: Let's go! I will accompany you.
Rajendra	: Get ready, my daughter! I am going to contact some people and arrange some guns for our journey.
Sambit	: Uncle, do you know how to shoot with a gun?
Rajendra	: (Laughs loudly)What do you mean? Wandering in the dense forest and hunting was my most favourite hobby. I used to shoot and drop flying birds. But I had stopped all these after the death of your aunt. Still, I have two guns and a revolver with me now. Now also I can shoot the target without fail.
Sambit	: Uncle! If you don't have any objection, I want to accompany you to the Himalayas.
Rajendra	: There is no question of me objecting. Instead, I will be happy. If you can spare some time, please come with us.
Sambit	: I have come prepared.
Rajendra	: Well, you please wait here at my place. I will make all kinds of arrangements shortly.
Lopa	: Come back soon, Dad!

Rajendra : While I arrange everything here, you inform your family, Lopa!

Lopa : Please don't bother about that. I will call my dad and inform him.
[Rajendra leaves.]

SCENE-III

[The location is the dense forest of the Himalayas. The rustling wind roars through the tress. Siddhartha is absorbed in deep meditation in the middle of the jungle. Rajendra, Sambit and Lopamudra sit calmly on a tree stand, close to his location.]

Lopa : How beautiful this tree stand is!

Sambit : You are right, Lopamudra! This tree stand surrounded by the beauty of nature is amazing. May be that's the reason why the birds are so happy. I never knew that living on a tree house would be so enticing.

Lopa : Really, it's breath taking! Loving this ambience.

Sambit : Siddhartha's choice is commendable. Look at the gurgling mountain stream moving slowly on the rocks. I am amazed by this medley of beautiful flowers surrounding us everywhere and the shadow of the dense trees covering the entire place like a large canopy hung on top.

Rajendra : I am grateful to you, Sambit! Had you not informed me at the right moment, I wouldn't have been able to successfully deploy these security guards around Siddharth.

Lopa	:	The place is full of wild creatures. Nature here is alluring and dreadful at the same time.
Sambit	:	Uncle, can you tell the name of the tree Siddhartha is siting under?
Rajendra	:	Is it necessary to know the name of that tree?
Sambit	:	Lopa Ma'am, can you tell the name of the tree under which the world-famous Siddhartha had achieved enlightenment?
Lopa	:	As long as I remember, that tree was *Bodhidruma*.
Sambit	:	If Siddhartha attains enlightenment, he will become a historical personality too. The tree under which he is meditating now will also get its name in the history. If we don't provide this information then how will history be written?
Lopa	:	This tree also looks like a Peepul tree.
Sambit	:	Peepul tree? No, how can a Peepul tree be seen in this dense forest?
Rajendra	:	The leaves of the tree are slightly larger than the peepul tree. I think they have grown bigger due to the fertile soil of this jungle. But no doubt, it's a Peepul tree, a wild one.
Lopa	:	Siddhartha has been meditating since four days. He has not taken any kind of food or beverages. It's obvious that he has gone weak. Still, he is determined and firm on his decision. Though he seems weak, his face blossoms with the mark of self-confidence.
Rajendra	:	Sambit! What you call self-confidence is only madness to me. The ghost of madness has captured him.

Sambit	: The actions of great personalities always seem insane to laymen. The day Prince Siddhartha gave up his royal throne, his kingdom, his wife, his son, people of his kingdom and got absorbed in meditation and austerity, people must have considered him a lunatic.
Rajendra	: Neither this place is Kapilavastu nor he is the prince. He is Siddhartha Choudhury, the only son of Rajendra Choudhury, the industrialist. Many centuries have passed after that. Modern science doesn't have any faith in meditation, austerity and enlightenment these days.
Sambit	: History repeats itself. Nobody can deny this.
Lopa	: (She starts yawning for sleep.)
Sambit	: Lopa Madam! Looks like you are feeling sleepy.
Lopa	: No, that's nothing. I can control myself.
Rajendra	: Lopa, you take some rest now. I will continue with the watch.
Lopa	: No, Dad! You have not slept at all for the last four days. Please, you sleep for a while. Sambit Babu and I are awake to keep a watch on him.
Sambit	: Yes, uncle, you seem very tired. Please, take rest.
Rajendra	: The night here is too dangerous, Sambit! There are lots of wild animals loitering around us. A little negligence can harm Siddhartha and all of us.
Lopa	: Along with us there are four troupes of security guards watching him closely from

		four different tree stands. They are alert, you please take rest.
Rajendra	:	They have kept their eyes on Siddhartha's safety. But if a tiger or a lion attacks on our tree stand when I am asleep then…
Sambit	:	Both Lopamudra and I have to learn how to fire a gun, though.
Rajendra	:	Fighting with a tiger or a lion with just a staff, knife, axe or dagger is dangerous. Don't worry about me. I can manage without sleep.
Sambit	:	Uncle!
Rajendra	:	What's it, Sambit?
Sambit	:	What's that above Siddhartha's head?
Rajendra	:	Where? Where's that?
Lopa	:	I can't see anything.
Sambit	:	Look at the direction of my finger. There. A small branch of the tree he is sitting under is bent over Siddharth's head. What's that hanging from the branch?
Lopa	:	That's the branch, nothing else.
Sambit	:	A branch or a snake?
Lopa	:	A snake!
Rajendra	:	Yes, yes, that looks like a snake.
Lopa	:	Oh my God! A Snake! Dad, please do something.
Sambit	:	We must do some thing immediately. Otherwise, it may harm Siddhartha.
Rajendra	:	I can shoot the snake dead from this tree stand.
Lopa	:	If you misfired by any chance, the snake will get startled and can harm Siddhartha.
Rajendra	:	My aim is flawless.

Sambit	:	Still, there is a risk for Siddhartha's life.
Rajendra	:	Then, what do we do now?
Lopa	:	Sambit Babu, do you have any other plan? Delaying it will be dangerous.
Sambit	:	No, I can't think of anything right now.
Lopa	:	If we throw some food towards the snake, it will get attracted. When it reaches for the food we can shoot it dead.
Sambit	:	But all of a sudden, from where will we get snake-food here? Snakes don't eat biscuits, rice or curry like us. For the snake…
Rajendra	:	These wild snakes roam around in the jungle hunting and consume enough food. They are not the hungry ones like the snakes living in the basket of a snake charmer. This wild snake will never get attracted towards food.
Sambit	:	Then, what do we do?
Lopa	:	Dad, see! The snake has started moving.
Rajendra	:	Yes, you are right. The snake is climbing down the tree slowly.
Sambit	:	There is a possibility that it may harm Siddhartha after climbing down.
Lopa	:	Yes, that is possible.
Rajendra	:	See, it is slithering away after hearing our voice. A snake never bites if you don't harm it. I guessed it right. It is leaving the spot.
Lopa	:	(Takes a deep breath) Oh my God! Siddhartha is safe now. There is no more danger.
Sambit	:	What kind of snake it is, Uncle?
Rajendra	:	I think it is none other than Python.
Sambit	:	I have heard a python can sometimes swallow a baby deer whole.
Rajendra	:	Yes, giant pythons can gulp down deers,

	goats, sheeps, cows, buffaloes, and stretch around trees later to digest them. Sometimes, they even swallow human beings.
Lopa	: Pythons are dangerous. They can be named wild beasts instead of snakes.
Rajendra	: Every single day, some or other kind of danger is threatening Siddhartha.
Sambit	: The attack of the wild elephants on the second day was far more dangerous than the attack of the bears on the first day.
Lopa	: Sambit Babu! I can smell something. A disgusting foul smell. [She spits and talks, closing her nose.]
Sambit	: (closes his nose) Yes, This one is a familiar smell. What is it?
Rajendra	: A tiger is somewhere nearby. I can smell its body odour.
Lopa	: Tiger! Oh, my goodness (Out of fear)!
Sambit	: Tigers are the most ferocious animals in this dense forest of the Himalayas.
Lopa	: I am really scared. What if the tiger plunges over our tree stand?
Sambit	: We can't negate that possibility.
Rajendra	: Don't be scared. I have hunted quite a lot of tigers in my time.
Lopa	: My knees are trembling out of fear. I have read in newspapers how tigers pounce on tree stands and eat the hunters alive.
Sambit	: If the tiger jumps, it can easily reach our tree stand. Besides that, tigers climbing trees are not something unheard of.
Rajendra	: If a tiger comes I will shoot it.
Lopa	: You can shoot and capture it if only one tiger

		comes, what if they come in groups?
Rajendra	:	Don't worry. First of all we will see how many of them are coming.
Sambit	:	How will we be sure of that? They will sneak up on us in the dense forest.
Lopa	:	My entire body is shivering.
Rajendra	:	Don't get scared. Sit calmly. Let me look into the matter.
Lopa	:	No, Dad! Don't leave us and go anywhere.
Sambit	:	(In a fearful voice) Ti…ger…tiger…tiger.
Lopa	:	(In a fearful voice) Where? Where is the tiger? Where?
Sambit	:	Look, it's there, glaring at us under that tree. [Meanwhile, the tiger roars. Lopa and Sambit cry out in fear.]
Rajendra	:	If you shout like this, it will be difficult for us to save ourselves from the tiger.
Sambit	:	I had never seen a wild tiger in the forest so closely. The tigers I have seen so far are the tamed ones in the circus.
Rajendra	:	I have a gun in my hand. We have got three troupes of armed guards watching us closely. Don't get afraid. The tiger can't harm us. Try to gaze at the tiger's eyes constantly without batting an eyelid.
Lopa	:	(Stammers in fear)My entire body is trembling with fear. I can't keep my eyes open.
Sambit	:	Look at the tiger! It is puffing its body and moustache, beating its tail and roaring loud. [A tiger's growl is heard.]
Rajendra	:	The tiger is frightening us. If we fall on the ground out of fear, it will pounce on us. Till

		the time we stand firmly staring at his eyes fearlessly, it won't harm us.
[The Tiger roars again.]
Lopa	:	Aim for the tiger's head and fire, Dad! It will jump on our tree stand if we delay anymore.
Sambit	:	Uncle! Please, shoot it. Fast.
Rajendra	:	No, it will be dangerous to fire the tiger unless we know whether it is alone or with the entire streak.
Lopa	:	That tiger has started moving.
Sambit	:	It is coming close to us. Uncle! Please shoot without any delay, otherwise it will eat all of us.
Rajendra	:	Fine. Both of you stay behind. (Targets the tiger with the gun.) I am aiming at the tiger. I will shoot once the tiger comes to my firing zone.
Sambit	:	Don't wait any more, Uncle! If it comes any closer, it may attack us.
Lopa	:	(Weeps) Dad, don't delay!
[The tiger roars.]
Rajendra	:	Don't worry, my child. I am ready.
[Rajendra fires at the tiger. The mixed sound of the gunshot is heard along with the tiger's roar and Siddharth's scream. After that, silence prevails for a while.]
Sambit	:	Looks like the tiger died after that roar. But we also have heard a human being howling along with that roar. Did the bullet passed through the tiger's body and hit someone present here?
Lopa	:	Where is Siddhartha?
Sambit	:	Hope Siddharth is not hit by the bullet?
Lopa	:	But that scream felt like Siddhartha's.

Sambit	: Uncle! Let's get down the tree stand. We are not sure what happened to Siddhartha. He is not there at the spot of his meditation.
Lopa	: Then, the bullet…
Rajendra	: No. It's not possible for the bullet to reach Siddharth. It is still stuck inside the tiger's head. Let's get down. We must find out where Siddhartha is.
Sambit	: Let's move, Uncle!
Rajendra	: Get hold of my hand, daughter! Yes, get down slowly. Take the support of the sidebars while climbing down.
Lopa	: Now leave me. I can get down alone.
Rajendra	: Yes, just two more steps and you are done!
Sambit	: Look, Siddhartha is coming towards us.
Lopa	: Are you fine, Siddhartha?
Siddhartha	: Yes, Lopa! I am safe.
Lopa	: Then, why did you shout like that?
Sambit	: Did the bullet touch your body?
Siddhartha	: Bullet? In my body?
Sambit	: That tiger was too violent, it tried to attack us. So, uncle shot it dead.
Lopa	: Yes, look, its dead body is laying here. Did the bullet pass through the tiger's body and hit you…by any chance?
Rajendra	: Lopa! Look at my hands. Neither they are weak nor do they tremble like the hands of an old man. Rajendra Choudhury's aim is flawless.
Sambit	: Why did you shout then if the bullet hasn't hit you?
Lopa	: I think the crack of the gunshot scared you and made you scream.

Siddhartha	:	No.
Rajendra	:	Then, why did you shout?
Siddhartha	:	I cried out in my dream.
Lopa	:	Were you dreaming in your meditation, then?
Siddhartha	:	While meditating, suddenly I saw myself gradually raising high above the ground along with my seat.
Sambit	:	Rising high means…? What was the height above the ground?
Siddhartha	:	Within a very short period, I entered the heavenly abode, travelling across a wide range of clouds in the sky. The divine brightness of the heaven lit up my eyes. [Flashback starts.] [A symbolic piece of music is heard when he enters the heaven.]
Siddhartha	:	How beautiful and exquisite this heaven is! Every single corner is spick and span. How enchanting are these beautiful towering palaces, lovely gardens, and velvety smooth royal highways! How beautiful these arches are! There are Deodar trees lined up on both the sides of the road. Just a single step on this divine soil excites me, unfurling the strings of my heart. Can our Earth be so beautiful like this ever? Oh, here! A divine person is coming towards me. Wow, how ravishingly handsome he is! His body is radiating rays of light. My eyes are sanctified, my life is blessed now. 'Pranam' my Lord!
Kubera	:	Get up, my child! I am not the Lord of the

	universe, I am Kubera, the God of Wealth. Who are you? You don't seem to be an inhabitant of heaven.
Siddhartha :	You guessed it right, your Majesty! I am from the Earth. My name is Siddhartha.
Kubera :	What is a man from the earth doing in the heaven? Any chance of conspiracy...
Siddhartha :	No, Lord Kubera! I don't have any evil intentions. I have come here in search of a truth. I hope you will help me in this regard. Kindly answer my queries and explain them.
Kubera :	Keeping somebody stand in the middle of the road and talking is not the kind of hospitality that we follow here in heaven. Please come; we can discuss it in the 'Garden of amusement'. We will sit in the lap of nature and talk. I will try my best to answer to all of your queries.
Siddhartha :	How far is the garden of amusement?
Kubera :	It's there, just ahead of us! Follow me. (The chirping of birds and the burbling song of the flowing stream is heard from a little distance.)
Kubera :	This is the garden of amusement. Be seated Siddharth! Sit here, on this bench.
Siddhartha :	Oh! What a wonderful garden adorned with a medley of colourful flowers, both exquisite and fragrant.
Kubera :	Now you can ask me your queries, Siddhartha!
Siddhartha :	I have heard that another name for heaven is Amaravati, the land of immortals. The Gods and Goddesses who reside here are

immortal. They live here happily after attaining forever youthfulness. I have come here in search of immortality and eternal youth for the humans of the earth. Please guide me on how to take all these from here to the earth.

Kubera : (laughs loudly)

Siddhartha : Why are you laughing my Lord? Did I say anything wrong?

Kubera : (Continues with his laughter)You will completely change your mind after staying here for a couple of days.

Siddhartha : I knew that the Gods are extreme opportunists. Please forgive me, I forget both the surroundings and myself while speaking the truth. My words may hurt you. I am very sorry for that.

Kubera : No, Siddhartha! You can speak your mind, freely, without any reservation or fear.

Siddhartha : Nowadays, the life span of human beings have increased to a certain extent due to the widespread application and promotion of science and technology on Earth. Still, life on Earth is uncertain. Sometimes, a man's life span falls short even to finish the meal served before him.

Kubera : Still, I can say human life is charming and beautiful.

Siddhartha : Life in heaven is true and eternal. But on earth, life is a lie and death is the ultimate truth. Life and youth are permanent in heaven, while both are transient on earth. Humans on earth live an uncertain life

	playing the game of hide-and-seek with life, youth and death.
Kubera	: You may say that an immortal life is exciting, but for us those who live this immortal life, it is excruciating and tiresome, like eternal death.
Siddhartha	: After a long period of practice and perseverance, what a skillful artist, a talented writer, or a world-famous scientist achieve is abruptly snatched away by death.
Kubera	: But, we have to carry the corpse of our lives on our shoulders and live this life forever till eternity. Our lives have no end, no boundary. For us, this deathless life is painful and unbearable. How miserable is a journey that has no destination!
Siddhartha	: But I can't understand you at all.
Kuber	: It's challenging to make a mortal man understand the plights of immortality in Amarapuri.
Siddhartha	: Please clarify. I need help understanding you.
Kubera	: There is no death here. And that's why there is no birth, too. When no one is taking birth here, there is no newness, no change in life. Look, Agnideva, the God of fire is approaching us.
Siddhartha	: I say 'Pranam', your Majesty!
Agni	: I bless you, keep shining!
Kubera	: Agnideva! Do you know who he is?
Agni	: No, I have not met him anywhere before. But his appearance says he belongs to the earth.
Kubera	: Yes, you are right.

Siddhartha	:	My name is Siddhartha.
Kubera	:	According to Siddhartha, since the habitants of heaven are immortal, they live a happy and prosperous life full of eternal youth and a deathless life. That's why he has come here for the humans on Earth, searching for them a long, prosperous, youthful life.
Agni	:	(Laughs loudly)Who says that life only is permanent here and death does not exist at all?
Siddhartha	:	The people on earth think that life is infinite here, there is no death in heaven. Death doesn't scare the Gods.
Agni	:	You are totally mistaken. I say, neither birth nor life has any existence here. Death, only death lives here.
Siddhartha	:	What for us is eternal life or immortality, how can that be active death for you?
Agni	:	We are tired of living a monotonous life since time immemorial. One may love to live for a hundred, two hundred or five hundred years, but Siddhartha, can you imagine how it feels to live crores and crores of years like us?
Kubera	:	You may think that this place is blessed with a death-less eternal life, but there lie the plights of death. We can't help you understand this. This can be felt and understood only through live experience.
Siddhartha	:	What is the problem for Gods in living and enjoying a life of everlasting youth for crores of years? This place also is bestowed with spring forever.

Agni	: All these you said are true, Siddhartha! But both immortal life and eternal spring are tiresome, unbearable and tasteless. We all do almost the same monotonous job every single day.
Kubera	: Everlasting youth is meaningless to us, as we have never experienced what old age is. Our body remains unaltered throughout. I am Dhanapati, the God of wealth, he is Agnideva, the God of fire, someone is Vidyapati, the God of knowledge, someone is Pabanadeva, the God of wind, and someone is Jaladev, the God of water. All our positions are fixed and roles are constant since the beginning of the creation.
Agni	: Life becomes more painful and irritating than death when you have to do the same job for ages. It would be better to say that living this type of a life is death only.
Kubera	: Life on your Earth is full of ups and downs, happiness, and sorrows. One can understand the value of life and enjoy it only if he experiences sadness and death in his life. If there is no sorrow, no death, then life seems boring and tiresome after a time. Subsequently, it becomes dull and dead.
Agni	: Every two months, seasons change on earth. Weather changes, the environment changes. Different seasons welcome different kind of fruits and vegetables, flowers, crops and cereals. But here, in the heaven…?
Kubera	: The spring season has persisted here in heaven for ages and will be here forever.

	The trees, plants, flowers, fruits, vegetables, and the ambience during spring are constant and so, they are mundane, unexciting and frustrating.
Kubera	: Life here is monotonous, youthfulness is definite, a single season continues forever and there is no change in the weather or in the ambience.
Kubera	: Life is not dynamic here but static, fixed, definite, stable, and never-changing.
Agni	: If anything is motionless and constant, that's not life but death.
Siddhartha	: But here in heaven, everything is available in abundance. You all live a life of luxury and prosperity. But the humans on earth rot in poverty and sufferings. Life no doubt is short-lived here on earth, but scarcity and misery make it even more painful and worse.
Agni	: One who experiences life in luxury and plentitude knows how repulsive it is. What is available in abundance, becomes boring and unexciting with time irrespective of its preciousness and beauty.
Kubera	: Life has no value for the one who has never tasted death. Similarly the one who doesn't know what old age is, can't feel the charm of youth. Someone who is not aware of the varied seasons of summer, autumn, dewy, winter, and rain can't enjoy the beautiful spring.
Agni	: He who hasn't experienced a life in poverty can't be amused by luxury.
Kubera	: The truth is that, in the name of an immor-

	tal life, we are experiencing death every moment, forever. There is no escape from this prison of life.
Agni	: Where there are no difficulties, no ups and downs, and no changes, how can one taste the sweetness of life there?
Kubera	: We, the inhabitants of heaven, are tired of bearing the load of luxury and plentitude.
Siddharth	: But humans feel the noose of death around their neck since their infancy. They can't even relish their short-lived lives in the fear of the approaching death. Throughout their lives they shiver with the fever of death. That fever in their body never goes down. And if in case the temperature drops, their bodies freeze, with the coldness of death.
Agni	: Death is beautiful. It is the road to freedom. A way to elude the pain and fatigues of life. A man suffering from the agonies of life firmly believes that one day, death will come and liberate him from this trap called life. In that hope only he gains some mental strength to face and tolerate pain and sorrow.
Kubera	: But that path is not open for the Gods. Their reliable path to escape from this entanglement of life is blocked forever.
Agni	: The inhabitants of heaven keep waiting for the arrival of death knowing very well that death is a rare, unattainable affair. They still earnestly hope that one day their darling death will come and liberate them from this monotonous life.
Siddhartha	: I accept that death frees one from the plights

	of life, but...
Kubera	: Again, what's this 'but', Siddhartha?
Siddhartha	: We will be ready to welcome 'Death' if we are empowered to remember our past lives. If humans can recollect all their previous lives, they will be able to use all their hard works, skills and accomplishments together and reach the peak of success.
Agni	: No, Siddhartha, no. Acquiring the power to remember our past lives is a curse. One who recollects the successes, hard works, skills and experiences of the previous lives also carries along the baggage of pain, sufferings, and troubles associated with those lives.
Kubera	: Apart from that, the baggage of that sorrow, sufferings, troubles and negative thoughts of the previous lives will become so heavy with time that he won't be able to stand straight in the present life .It will break his backbone and hobble his walk.
Agni	: Besides that, the man who can remember the past lives will not fear death. One who is not afraid of death will have no fear of anything. A life without fear is indisciplined. That man will breach the laws of the social system. Such an unruly life will be a problem on Earth.
Siddhartha	: If you all are arguing so much in favour of a man living on earth, then why don't you come along with me and live there? Come and enjoy your life there.
Agni	: We don't always get the chance to live on earth. But whenever any of us, the

	inhabitants of heaven, get that opportunity we don't miss the boat.
Kubera	: We have taken birth at different points in time on earth. We still fondly remember those few days we were able to spend there. The opportunity to take birth on earth itself is like a temporary death for us from this monotonous life in heaven.
Agni	: We feel relieved from this mundane life of heaven until we live on earth. That gives us a chance to experience the taste of death.
Kubera	: Ah! How peaceful those days staying on earth were!
Agni	: How beautiful and amazing the earth is!
Kubera	: Why are you silent, Siddhartha? Tell us what more you need.
Siddhartha	: I want to meet the Lord of the Universe, Bhagwan Vishnu before I decide anything. Please make some arrangements for a meeting with him.
Agni	: All right. It won't look nice to return from the heaven without meeting Lord Vishnu. Come with us. We will take an appointment for you to meet the Lord accordingly. But you have to wait for a while outside.
Kubera	: Lord Vishnu's meeting hall is always crowded. He is always busy. We, the deities, also wait outside the entrance most of the time to meet Him.
Siddhartha	: I know that. I am ready to wait outside.
Agni	: Fine then, you come, Siddhartha! Lord Kuber, please, you also join in.

Kubera	:	Let's go.
		[First flashback ends.]
Lopa	:	What happened after that?
Sambit	:	Did you follow them to meet Lord Vishnu in the *Vaikunthapur, the abode of Lord Vishnu*?
Siddhartha	:	Yes, I reached *Vaikunthapur* in that dream following Lord Agni and Lord Kuber. But the security guard stopped me at the door.
Sambit	:	Agni Dev and Kubera Dev must have helped you enter inside.
Siddhartha	:	They told me- 'Siddhartha! Wait here at the door. You can meet Lord Vishnu, after we take permission from Him. I sat there following their instructions. Agni Dev and Kubera Dev went to Lord Vishnu for permission.
		[The second flashback starts.]
		[Location- *Vaikunthapur*. Lord Vishnu is seen sleeping in his *Anantāsana*. Agni Dev and Kubera Dev stand nearby.]
Vishnu	:	Oh! Agni Dev! Kubera Dev! When did you arrive? Please come and have your seats.
Kubera	:	Pranam!The Lord of Vaikuntha!
Agni	:	Pranam! The Lord of Vaikuntha!
Vishnu	:	Is everything fine in heaven?
Kubera	:	Everything is fine here with your blessings, My Lord!
Vishnu	:	Do you have any special message for me? How is that both of you are here at an odd time?
Agni	:	No, Sir! There is no special news. Only…
Vishnu	:	Express yourself freely without any inhibition.
Agni	:	A young man has come here from earth. He wants to meet you.

Vishnu	:	Where is he?
Kubera	:	He is waiting outside the door.
Vishnu	:	Please get him to me.
Agni	:	All right. I will go get him. (Exits)
Vishnu	:	Why is the man from the earth here?
Kubera	:	You are *Antaryāmi*; you know everything, My Lord!
Vishnu	:	(Smiles) Still…
Kubera	:	What is this 'still', Your Majesty! He is already here. He himself will tell you the reason of his arrival in the heaven.
Siddhartha	:	(Enters and touches Lord Vishnu's feet.) Pranam, My Lord!
Vishnu	:	Get up, my child! Spell out your reason for visiting heaven.
Siddharth	:	I have come to heaven in search of the immortal life for the humans on our planet. But I have to return empty-handed.
Vishnu	:	Agni Dev! Have you not told the real fact to this young man?
Agni	:	Both Kubera Dev and I have made him understand everything clearly.
Siddhartha	:	Kubera Dev and Agni Dev have enlightened me with the reality and have opened my eyes of wisdom.
Kubera	:	After all those realizations also he wants something more.
Agni	:	I also feel so. It's not only about this young man, every single person on earth has a latent desire to attain an immortal life. That's because there is no place more enchanting than the earth.
Siddhartha	:	An immortal life seems terrible because of

		the never ending pain of life. We don't need the immortal life if what Kubera Dev and Agni Dev told me are correct.
Vishnu	:	Then, what's the reason for your visit to me?
Siddhartha	:	If possible, please bless us with an immortal life without pain and fatigue, my Lord!
Kubera	:	How can that be possible? If one lives permanently, he will have to bear the agonies and weariness of life.
Agni	:	You should not request for something that is not attainable.
Vishnu	:	There is a way Siddharth!
Siddhartha	:	(In a Happy mood) Is it so, My Lord? Kindly tell me without any delay!
Vishnu	:	Man must do some noble work during the limited time he is on earth which will make him immoral in the minds of all forever. That kind of immortality is free of pain or languor. Instead, it has pride and glory. When there is a throng of these kind of great and noble souls on the earth, the earth will change into heaven. Nobody will come to heaven searching for immortal life.
Siddhartha	:	I am grateful to you, My Lord! You have advised me rightly. I am enlightened. I am blessed for my dedication and hard work. I am really happy and satisfied today. Let me return to earth, please give me the permission.
Vishnu	:	Why are you in a hurry to return to earth?
Siddhartha	:	I have already ruined a lot of days from my lifespan wandering here and there. I don't want to waste a moment unnecessarily. I am

	very anxious to return to my beautiful earth immediately.
Vishnu	: All right! When you are so eager to return immediately to the earth, I will make the arrangement for the same. Kubera Dev! Tell Indra Dev to arrange for this young man to reach the earth by *Puspak Viman* (mythological flying chariot).
Kubera	: I will pass your order to Devraj Indra as soon as possible.
Siddhartha	: No, there is no need for all this, Lord! I can manage it myself. Pranam, my Lord! Pranam Kubera Dev and Agni Dev! (He tries to jump from heaven to Earth.)
Kubera	: Siddhartha! What are you doing?
Agni	: Don't try to jump from such a height, Siddhartha!
Kubera	: Siddhartha! Siddhartha!! Don't jump from such a height.

[Without giving a heed to others, Siddhartha jumps from heaven to earth. While he jumps, a background musical effect like the fall of a rocket is heard playing. Siddhartha shouts after falling on the ground.]

[The second flashback ends.]

Lopa	: Siddhartha! Are you in your senses, or still wandering the dreamland?
Siddhartha	: Lopa!
Lopa	: Does your research end here, or you still plan to absorb yourself in meditation? Why are you silent now Siddharth?
Rajendra	: Forget all this madness and concentrate on your work. It does not look nice for an

	educated young man like you to meditate here like an ascetic. For how long I will be able to take care of this house and the factory alone?
Sambit	: Siddhartha! Are you interested to do more research on the truth that you saw or the knowledge you gained in your dream?
Siddhartha	: No, Sambit! I have gained knowledge of the truth from my research. Though it was a dream, it was the reality for me. That dream has introduced the subtle, mysterious fact between life and death before me. My research ends successfully.
Lopa	: Siddhartha!
Siddhartha	: I am delighted, Lopa! I am so happy that it is difficult for me to express my happiness neither in words and nor in action.
Rajendra	: Siddhartha!
Siddhartha	: I feel guilty before you, Dad! I have hurt you and compelled you to come to the Himalayas, at this age. Can't you forgive me, Dad?
Sambit	: The heart of a father is like the sea, vast and generous. He becomes great when he forgives all the mistakes of his son.
Rajendra	: Sambit is right, Siddhartha! You have not committed any crime. Instead, you have been enlightened by your research. I am proud of you for that.
Siddhartha	: Lopa! I have hurt your innocent heart by discrediting your love, affection and care. Still, you have not rejected me, instead you have come to this dense forest for my safety and security, putting your life in danger. Your love has completely moved and hypnotized

	me, Lopa! I hope you will forgive me.
Lopa	: You are, to me, another Siddhartha. After gaining enlightenment, the history-famous Siddhartha of Kapilvastu didn't return to his wife, Yashodhara. But my Siddhartha has returned to me after enlightenment. I am excited about that happiness.
Sambit	: The message of Kapilvastu's Siddhartha was : The world is full of sorrows and suffering; Desire is the root cause of this suffering; the end to desire ends the sorrows and leads one to salvation or nirvana. But what's the message of this Siddhartha?
Siddhartha	: This Earth is beautiful and incomparable. Here, sorrow glorifies happiness, old age romanticizes youth, and death magnifies life. So, if all the individuals, without fearing death, do noble and virtuous deeds within their limited lifespan, they will be immortal, and their lives will be glorified. When everybody will attain immortality doing noble works, one day this earth full of dust will turn heaven.

[After Siddharth's speech, with a grave tone, the following *śloka* is recited from the background.]

"Duhkha binā nahi kadāpi sukhānubhūtih, mrutyu binā madhuram jananasya mūlyam tasmād bibarttana parā dharani suranam kamya, sadaika bidhi chalita devapurvā."

END

Black Eagle Books

www.blackeaglebooks.org
info@blackeaglebooks.org

Black Eagle Books, an independent publisher, was founded as a nonprofit organization in April, 2019. It is our mission to connect and engage the Indian diaspora and the world at large with the best of works of world literature published on a collaborative platform, with special emphasis on foregrounding Contemporary Classics and New Writing.

www.ingramcontent.com/pod-product-compliance
Lightning Source LLC
Chambersburg PA
CBHW021627080526
44585CB00013BA/827